Multicultural Education in the United States

MULTICULTURAL EDUCATION IN THE UNITED STATES

David E. Washburn

with
Neil L. Brown
and
Robert W. Abbott

Inquiry International
Philadelphia

Produced, Edited, and Designed by DANIEL C. WASHBURN
Cover Design by SAM BIDLEMAN

Printed in the United States of America.

Library of Congress Catalog Card Number 96-77221

ISBN 0-9635521-2-0

 Inquiry International
Business Office, 7015 Scenic Drive, Bloomsburg, PA 17815
Editorial Office, 1203 Brighton Street, Philadelphia, PA 19111

This book is printed on acid-free paper.

CONTENTS

LIST OF TABLES

INTRODUCTION

A Conceptual Framework for
Multicultural Education[1]

THE TERM **CULTURE** REFERS TO THE TOTAL WAY OF LIFE OF A PEOPLE WHICH makes them distinctive. This *way of life* is based upon a set of tradition-derived norms which influence the behavior of the people subject to them. The people who grow up within a particular cultural context have been subjected to the same patterned system and therefore share a common view of the world. Their language, values, attitudes, beliefs, and behaviors tend to be similar.

Although the stated ideal of the United States has, for many years, been the assimilation of all of its people into a common **melting pot**, some minority groups have not fully penetrated the system of power and influence sometimes referred to as the mainstream of the society. Our society, therefore, although having an identifiable **mainstream culture**, is more accurately regarded as being culturally pluralistic. That is, a number of very distinct cultural groups exist as separate parts of the total society.

An ideal form of **cultural pluralism** would include: different cultural groups existing in the same society while maintaining their cultural identities; having mechanisms for easy interaction with one another and equal opportunity of access to the institutions of that society; as well as

1

equal opportunity for participation in the formation of the values which regulate that society.

Clearly, as is true with the melting pot **ideology**, we have not actualized an ideal form of cultural pluralism. What does exist in our country is a society which is, by and large, segregated along lines of color and culture.

What does this mean for children growing up in our society?

Children first learn their cultures, the language patterns they will employ, their values, attitudes, beliefs, and acceptable behaviors from their families. As they grow, they begin to internalize their cultures and act in the manner their cultures dictate, without being consciously aware of it. The cultural patterns they learn become their own, inseparable from their own personalities. This process is called **enculturation**. Through interaction with their families and other members of their cultural groups the values of the cultures are transmitted to them.

In our society the family is a major agent of enculturation—from the birth of children through their early school years. Other important agents through which children learn their cultures and come to have self-identities are schools, religious organizations, peer groups, and the mass media, especially television.

These agents and other institutions in the society may act either to reinforce the process of enculturation through which children are gaining identities, or may interrupt the process, produce cultural discontinuities, and lead children to question their cultures and their self-worth.

As children grow older, families exert an increasingly less powerful enculturative influence, and the peer group a more powerful one. The school, as both an institution through which culture is transmitted and as a vehicle for peer group interaction, can have a strong influence on the growth of children.

Although the nature of education in our society is changing as schools come to grips with the realities of cultural diversity in our pluralistic society, the traditional culture of the school is that of the mainstream. The school is itself a cultural system. It teaches and expects a particular language, certain values, attitudes, and beliefs. It rewards certain behaviors and punishes others.

If the school teaches and expects a certain conformity with mainstream culture, in what ways does this affect children whose cultures are different from the mainstream?

It certainly places an additional burden upon them, for, if they are to succeed in terms of the school's definition of success, they must learn to understand a cultural pattern different from the one they have learned in their homes and develop mechanisms for accommodating to it. They are forced to **acculturate**, to adapt to a dominant culture other than their own.

While, for those children coming from families that are part of the mainstream culture, the school experience is simply one of a continuation of the transmission of the cultural patterns begun in the home; for children whose cultures are different from the mainstream, an entirely new mode of perception and behavior is required. The first days of school can be a traumatic experience for any child. Imagine the degree of trauma that may result when children enter an unfamiliar institution which utilizes and demands a language pattern and code of behavior which is totally unfamiliar to them. These children, **culturally different** children, are certainly at a disadvantage, a **cultural disadvantage**, in this setting.

Children who are forced into an acculturative experience upon entering school may become successful in school in either of two ways. They may **assimilate**. That is, they may relinquish their former sets of cultural traits and acquire the traits of the mainstream culture. On the other hand, they may become truly **bicultural**. That is, they may learn to retain their own cultural identities while also being capable of operating effectively and with a minimum amount of anxiety in the mainstream culture.

Children who assimilate lose a culture. They may no longer feel at ease in it. They will lose communication with their former cultures and families and former friends who retain the original culture. Children who become truly bicultural gain a culture, but not without a large expenditure of psychic energy. They must become successfully schizoid. They must know, understand, and be able to employ the correct set of cultural traits at appropriate times. They may have to be **bilingual** or **bidialectal**. They must know which forms of behavior are acceptable in each setting and be able to respond according to the expectations of the group they are with.

Although assimilation or biculturality on the part of the minority group student may be a prerequisite for success in school, it is no *guarantee* of success in school or in the world beyond the school. For this to occur, the mainstream culture must be willing to accept the culturally different individual as a fully participating member.

If assimilated or bicultural minority group persons are not provided access to the mainstream culture, what are their options? They have already gone through a transformation of self. They have been forced to create an identity with which they were not armed upon approaching society's agent of mainstream culture—the school. Truly bicultural individuals may be able to achieve some solace through withdrawal to the minority group culture while dealing with the frustration of being less than a full-fledged member of the broader society in which they live. Maybe not. But what of assimilated individuals? They have bought the American Dream. Where have they to go, having lost a culture while being banned from entry into the culture for which they are prepared? They join their brothers and sisters who failed to acculturate in the first place. Those individuals without a culture who have lost personal identities...whose self-images are confused. They become **marginal** individuals living on the illusive margin between cultures, people without homes.

There is a high index of crime, family disorganization, and emotional disturbance among the marginal members of our society. Some, in search of self, groping for an identity, join or form movements in which distinctive modes of dress and behavior are demanded. The goals of such groups are generally aimed toward the destruction of the mainstream culture which stripped them of their identities in the first place.

There are others, of course, who, having lost the battle of acculturation early, or having demurred from the contest, don't attempt to penetrate the dominant culture, but do operate effectively within their own cultural contexts. It is highly unlikely, however, that the culturally different individual will go through life unscarred by the trauma of hostile cross-cultural contact.

What are we, the elders of the society, to do if we wish to make a better life for *all* of our children?

Most often we look to the public school as an agent for the solution of our social problems. We have high expectations of performance for our schools. Witness the amount of energy our society expends in criticism of the public schools of our nation. Certainly the public school is an important foundation upon which the future of our society rests. It is regarded as a microcosm of the broader society through which the ideals of that society may be reached. The orientation of the society's view of the school is toward the future. It is in the school that we visualize our hopes and aspirations for the future of our society.

It is to the school, therefore, that we look for the solutions to the problems involved in the issues of color and culture. The school is the setting in our society in which people of diverse cultural backgrounds come into the most intimate contact. It is here that we must gain an understanding of our differences, make use of them for further understanding, and begin to develop a new nation which will more closely approximate the ideals of democracy.

Many reason that since we live in a culturally pluralistic society, the school curriculum should reflect this fact. Elements of a variety of cultures should be essential ingredients in the experience of each school child. The study of these cultures should be a required part of the public school curriculum.

Further, teaching methods should be grounded in a thorough understanding of the cultural backgrounds of the children. To reach students, teachers must understand the languages or dialects they employ, be aware of their experiential backgrounds, and utilize strategies and materials which children perceive as relevant to their lives.

Through this process, all children could become bicultural, rather than marginal. At least they should understand and be tolerant of people with cultural orientations different from their own.

It follows, therefore, that teacher education should have as a major focus multicultural education. Teachers should be made aware of cultural differences and the implications of these differences for classroom practice. Teachers should be able to adjust their styles, the content of their subject matters, and the materials they use to suit the students they teach.

The content of a teacher education curriculum should include aspects which will sensitize teachers to their own personal and cultural identities as well as to the identities of others. Certification requirements should include work in multicultural education and inter-ethnic relations. This should entail pre-practicum conceptual content as well as face to face practicum experience in diverse cultural settings. Education scholars should continue to proceed apace in the development of administrative structures, curricular designs, instructional strategies, and materials which can be used with effect in the multicultural school and hasten to provide training in their use.

CHAPTER ONE

Multicultural Education: Origins, Development, and Prospects[1]

MULTICULTURAL EDUCATION IS A STRATEGY FOR SCHOOLING WHICH utilizes the concept of democratic pluralism as a standard for designing administrative, instructional, and curricular models. Rooted in the principles of a culturally pluralistic nation whose ideals are stated in democratic terms, multicultural education recognizes that liberty, justice, and equality of opportunity are values which should encompass all of our peoples. If imbalances exist between the ideals of democratic pluralism and the reality of social organization in the United States, multiculturalists reason that a school committed to these ideals should endeavor as best it can to right the imbalances by producing in its students a regard for the rights of others and a desire that these values be reached.

William Greenbaum argued for the ideals of democratic pluralism when he wrote:

> Support for positive...multicultural identities will encourage not only renewed respect for this country but also the development of true universalism, in which the merits and faults of different belief systems can be more intelligently assessed because the individual and the group deeply understand more than one culture...by taking

responsibility for our own institutions and communities, all of us could better develop our capabilities for self-governance and better understand how the traditions we have inherited or created can be positively linked to those modern institutional forms that are worth saving...Culturally appropriate institutions could be created to deliver social services with more respect, equity, and effectiveness...there is the likelihood that a stronger and more humane individualism can be built in concert with cultural pluralism. Finally, pluralism must be respected because for many Americans ineradicable cultural and linguistic diversity already exists and provides ample foundations for strong institutions and communities.[2]

At the time Greenbaum expressed this opinion, recognition of the culturally pluralistic nature of the United States as expressed in school practices was an emergent, and not modal, phenomenon. The assimilationist mentality, a belief that all of society's children should blend into a mainstream, had, over the generations, firmly rooted itself in school practices which were based upon Anglo-Saxon values.

Although a number of nonpublic schools originally formed for the purposes of preserving a cultural heritage outside of the mainstream have retained non-assimilationist administrative, instructional, and curricular practices over the years[3], for the most part multicultural education in the public schools was just beginning.

The term *cultural pluralism* was introduced in 1915 by Horace M. Kallen.[4] The concept of *culture*, the total way of life of a people which makes them distinctive, did not begin to have wide impact on educational thought and practice until the early 1960s, however. The idea that children's perceptions, behaviors, languages, attitudes, beliefs, and learning styles are dependent upon the cultural context within which they are brought up, that differences abound in our culturally pluralistic society, and *that schools and teachers should pay homage to this fact in the practices they employ* were relatively new concepts for public school education which received major impetus during the 1970s.

As is so often the case in education, the impact of new ideas was directly tied to the amount of funding available for the development of programs. It is said that President John F. Kennedy was considerably moved by Michael Harrington's book *The Other America*[5], which was written in 1961 and published in 1962. In it, Harrington described a "culture of poverty." John Kennedy began, and Lyndon Johnson announced in 1964, a "war on poverty." Studies were initiated with federal support during the Kennedy Administration which related membership in the "culture of poverty" with the school performance of children.

A review of educational literature will indicate that the term *culture* does not begin to appear with any regularity until 1962[6], following Oscar Lewis' juxtapositioning of the term with "poverty."[7] The notion of a "culture of poverty" began to inform educational thinkers on this topic. Unfortunately, with the best of intentions (the amelioration of deficits produced by "poor" backgrounds), the concept most closely associated with culture in the literature of the period was that of "deprivation." Therefore, what one finds is a burgeoning literature of "cultural deprivation" during the mid-1960s. This was unfortunate because those groups most devastated by poverty, in terms of the percentages of their total populations, were the minority cultures.

In terms of raw numbers there were, and are, more white people living in poverty than any other group, but the concept of "deprivation" of a cultural heritage which negatively influenced school performance seems to have been most readily applied to non-white children.

It is apparent from reviewing the literature of "cultural deprivation" that the assimilationist mentality prevailed in education. These children exhibited differences in terms of values, attitudes, behaviors, and language and learning styles from those expected and rewarded in schools which institutionalized Anglo-Saxon, middle-class, mainstream culture. The problem was initially perceived as how to change the children, not how to change the schools.

During this period, the movement for Civil Rights was gaining momentum. Its impact on education began with studies which uncovered the Anglo-Saxon, middle-class bias which existed in school curricula, materials, and practices. In the early 1960s John Chilcott conducted an analysis of the cultural values promulgated by elementary school reading materials from the *McGuffy Reader* to books used at the time.[8] Although the orientation had changed over the years, it reflected internal changes in middle-class attitudes rather than recognition of cultural pluralism. Whereas the *McGuffy Reader* stressed a work-success theme, a heavy church orientation, the Protestant Puritan ethic, and character building, the early 1960s reading materials portrayed an upper-middle class suburban life-style: an aseptically clean suburban home; a large green lawn; a father dressed in a business suit with white shirt and tie; a mother who picked up toys; a child-centered environment in which daddy, the provider of material objects for a "good" life, brought home toys; an emphasis on cleanliness, consumption, materialism, and glamour; white faces everywhere.

These materials, and the values which generated them, became a focal point for concern by organized minority groups. The concept of "cultural deprivation" also chafed. Although many could see that their children were at a disadvantage in a school which institutionalized a culture different from their own, they did not see their children—African American, Mexican American, Puerto Rican, Cuban American, Asian American, Native American, and others—as having been denied a rich cultural heritage.

A movement began for including those American heritages in school curricula along with the Anglo-Saxon heritage which had for so long prevailed. The political and social pressure applied by these groups helped change the face of American education and educational materials. Publishers who initially simply sprinkled some brown and black faces among those pictured in their materials, while maintaining the same cultural biases in the content, began developing legitimately multicultural products. Schools, in increasing numbers, developed administrative, instructional, and curricular strategies aimed at reflecting the culturally pluralistic nature of the country. And, many national, state, and local organizations supported multicultural education.[9]

A 1974 survey of the 720 public school districts in the United States which served student populations of 10,000 or more revealed the extent to which various kinds of multicultural education were being practiced at that time.[10] Of the 397 school districts (55.1%) reporting practices designed to produce multi-ethnic understanding, the most common were: an **ethnic studies** curriculum (72.5%); human relations training for teachers (66.8%); a strong school-community public relations effort (52%); and inservice teacher training in multicultural education (49.4%). Other strategies used by some of the school systems included: student involvement in curriculum planning (44.8%); instruction in Spanish as a second language (43.6%); student involvement in school policy decisions (40.6%); an inter-racial student council (37%); a multicultural curriculum (36%); instruction in English as a second language (34%); human relations training for students (32%); a professionally staffed community relations office (29.2%); a community centered instructional program (26.7%); a bilingual curriculum (26.2%); a professionally staffed human relations team (22.9%); a student human relations council (21.2%); a bicultural curriculum (17.4%); a multilingual curriculum (7.8%); instruction in standard English as a second dialect (5.8%); instruction in Asian languages as second languages (4.5%); and instruction in Native American languages as second languages (2.3%).[11]

The pivotal factor in determining a school district's overall commitment to multicultural education appeared to be the inclusion of an ethnic studies curriculum. The 288 systems reporting such a curriculum were much more likely to include other elements of multicultural education than those which did not.[12]

This 1974 study also showed that fully 81.7% of the ethnic studies curricula had been established since 1969. Only twelve districts (4.2%) indicated having had a program for ten or more years.

Among the 40% of the school districts with ethnic studies curricula, African Americans (92%), Mexican Americans (70.5%), Native Americans (67%), Japanese Americans (49.3%), Chinese Americans (43.1%), and Puerto Ricans (34.4%) were the groups most often included. The history of the groups was the most commonly studied feature. Social customs, culture and personality, values, attitudes, material culture, social organization, beliefs, religion, and language were other elements included by at least half of the programs.[13]

Undoubtedly there were regional differences in the extent to which various groups were included. For example, in Pennsylvania's public school systems, although the study of African American and Native American heritages approached the national averages, those reporting ethnic studies curricula included German (including Pennsylvania Dutch) studies at a much higher rate (50.4% in Pennsylvania to 29.9% nationally) and Mexican American studies at a much lower rate (41.1% in Pennsylvania to 70.5% nationally).[14]

Clearly, however, the efforts of organized minority groups in the late 1960s and early 1970s had a massive impact upon public school education in the United States. A few states enacted legislation mandating multicultural education through regulations, guidelines, resolutions, or policy statements.

For example, the Pennsylvania Department of Education had a person assigned to ethnic studies; mandated a bilingual education program; and produced materials in multicultural education, ethnic studies, human relations training, and bilingual/bicultural education.[15] As well, the Commonwealth of Pennsylvania, through legislation, supported the Pennsylvania Ethnic Heritage Studies Center located at the University of Pittsburgh. This was a resource center which conducted workshops in ethnic studies, published an ethnic studies newsletter, and produced ethnic studies materials.[16]

States which had legislation mandating multicultural education included California, Florida, Illinois, Iowa, Minnesota, Ohio, and Wisconsin.[17] Massachusetts, like Pennsylvania, had State Department of Education regulations for multicultural education, while Michigan offered State Department of Education guidelines. Other states with provisions for multicultural education included Arkansas, Oregon, and West Virginia.[18]

Many state departments of education and local school districts had produced materials for their ethnic studies programs. A good number of these materials were available for purchase.[19] A range of bibliographies had been produced which could have assisted teachers wishing to develop ethnic studies components for their classes.[20] Directories of programs and personnel were published.[21] These directories offered program models and identified consultants and locally produced materials.

Much of this latter activity gained impetus from the 1972 passage of Title IX of the Elementary and Secondary Education Act. As a result of Title IX legislation funding for training of persons in ethnic studies, curriculum materials development, and dissemination of materials in ethnic studies was begun in 1974.[22]

Although in many state departments of education and school systems the initial emphasis was placed on "minority studies,"[23] a broad spectrum of **ethnic groups** began clamoring for representation in school curricula. Following the lead of the organized minority groups, whose impact was felt in the 1960s, other groups, under-represented in school programs, began to make inroads. The mid- and late-1970s saw the rise of the "unmeltable ethnics" in terms of school curricula. Slavic, Italian, Irish, and other heritage groups who make up the American mosaic were increasingly concerned that their American histories and their sensibilities be included in the education of all school children. In 1974 they and other groups were included in a minority of the curricula of the 288 large public school systems which had ethnic studies programs (e.g., Italian Americans [31.3%], German Americans [29.9%], Irish Americans [29.5%], French Americans [26%], Polish Americans [25%], Russian Americans [20.5%]).[24]

Also, in general, there appeared to be a new search for identity among the American people. More and more Americans began searching for their roots. Many found them in a new sense of ethnicity. Americanism and pride in a pre-American heritage came to be seen as compatible entities. And, importantly, the school was being perceived as a vehicle for fostering a new American ideal—pluralism.

In addition to the support from the federal sector through the Title IX program, the American Association of Colleges for Teacher Education, the Association for Supervision and Curriculum Development, the National Council for the Social Studies, the National Association of Elementary School Principals, the National Association of Secondary School Principals, the Council of Chief State School Officers, and the American Association of School Administrators took positions favorable to multicultural education.[25] Many of these organizations were very active in seeing that school programs and practices were representative of the culturally pluralistic nature of our nation.

Significantly, the National Council for the Accreditation of Teacher Education in their 1979 Standards placed strong emphasis on multicultural education in the content and conduct of teacher education programs. For this reason, as much as any, the future of multicultural education looked bright.

As an expression of the confidence at least one author had in the notion that multicultural education would burgeon in the years ahead, in an article published in 1979, David E. Washburn wrote:

> Perhaps a measure of the success of the movement toward multicultural education during the 1970s may be found in the fact that a backlash movement is developing against it. Articles are beginning to appear in respected educational journals which question the validity of multicultural education and rumblings of discontent with the 1979 National Council for the Accreditation of Teacher Education Standards are emanating from colleges of teacher education.

> The ensuing debate, which no doubt will occur in the last years of the decade, may galvanize the disparate voices favoring a culturally pluralistic orientation for the schools. It should force the development of a fully articulated theory of multicultural education which is now lacking. It should lead to the development of increasing numbers of multidisciplinary-multiethnic curricula encompassing all ethnic groups and all grade levels. And, it should make the 1980s an exciting period for those involved in multicultural education, perhaps ultimately leading to a realization of a new American Dream.[26]

However, during the 1980s those who dreamed of a democratic, egalitarian, pluralistic transformation of the United States through progressive, reconstructionist, multicultural education were confronted with the essentialist, assimilationist, **anglo-conformist** reforms of the *A Nation At Risk* report and promulgated by William Bennett, Allan Bloom, and many others. The backlash Washburn wrote of became educational policy during the Reagan-Bush years and efforts at establishing multicultural education in the nation's public schools appeared to wane.

The backlash and culture clash continues, but, the demographic realities are that Los Angeles and San Antonio now have "minority majorities"—populations of African Americans, Hispanic Americans, and Asian Americans, which when combined, outnumber the white population. Other cities will soon follow. By the next century members of minority groups will be the majority of the overall United States population.[27] As a result of the realization of this fact by policy makers as well as a growing body of scholarship, attention to the issue by publishers, and other factors, multicultural education is having a resurgence in the 1990s.

CHAPTER TWO

Multicultural Education:
Conceptions and Descriptions

I
F WE ARE TO RECONCEPTUALIZE MULTICULTURAL EDUCATION FOR THE twenty-first century, a descriptive analysis and critical evaluation of multicultural education as it presently stands is in order. No national descriptive studies of multicultural education policy and practice have been conducted since Washburn's mid-1970s surveys of the 720 largest school districts in the United States, all of the public school districts and private schools in Pennsylvania, and all institutions of higher education in the country.[1] So, a descriptive analysis and critical evaluation of contemporary multicultural education must entail an analysis and evaluation of *conceptions* of multicultural education which have appeared in the literature on the topic as well as a survey of the state of the art as practiced in the public schools. Our working hypothesis is that much education that is multicultural can be found in urban areas whereas, the suburban and rural practices of this orientation are problematic.

CONCEPTIONS OF MULTICULTURAL EDUCATION
Sleeter and Grant[2] have provided a useful typology of conceptions of multicultural education breaking schooling down to *business as usual*

and five approaches to multicultural education: *teaching the exceptional and culturally different, human relations, single-group studies, multicultural education,* and *education that is multicultural and social reconstructionist.* Since their analysis has been influential in providing a framework for investigation of multicultural education and many in the field are familiar with their typology, it will be utilized in the analysis of conceptions and descriptions of multicultural education.

According to the Sleeter and Grant typology **business as usual** is traditional, teacher-centered education with little accommodation to differing student learning styles or individualization. Teachers utilizing this approach focus their attention on the white, male, and middle-class students more than others in the same classroom. The curriculum is Euro-centric in spite of the availability of materials which reflect cultural diversity. Neighborhood schools tend to be unidimensional in terms of ethnicity and **social class**. Grouping and tracking in more heterogeneous settings resegregates students along racial, ethnic, gender, and social class lines. Students in the different tracks and groups are treated differently with lower expectations being maintained for ethnic minority students. In general the patterns in the *business as usual* settings mirror and reproduce the **race**, social class, and gender patterns of the broader society.[3]

Schools operating from the **teaching the exceptional and culturally different** approach try to fit students into the existing social structure and culture. They teach lower-class, minority, special education, limited-English proficiency, or female students who are behind in the main school subjects' traditional subject matter by building on students' learning styles and adapting to their skill levels. They attempt to make traditional subject matter relevant to students' experiential backgrounds. The focus is on integration of the exceptional and culturally different students into mainstream society by involving their parents in supporting the work of the school and using transitional bilingual education, English as a second language, remedial classes, and special education to this end.[4]

The societal goal of those advocating the **human relations** approach is to promote feelings of unity, tolerance, and acceptance among people within the existing social structure. In school they try to promote positive feelings among all students by reducing stereotyping and to enhance students' self-concepts. They utilize cooperative learning and student experiences in teaching lessons about stereotyping, individual differences, and the contributions to society made by members of various groups. In general, this orientation promotes classroom and school themes which promote the general human welfare.[5]

Single-group studies promote social structural equality for and immediate recognition of the identified group. They call on all students to work for change that would benefit a particular group. They employ faculty who are group members and utilize the learning style of the group in teaching about the group, their history of victimization, and current issues involving the group from the group's point of view. Classrooms are decorated to reflect the group. Representatives of the group are asked to become involved in class activities as guest speakers and resource persons.[6]

According to Sleeter and Grant, advocates of **multicultural education** wish to promote social structural equality and cultural pluralism in the society and equal opportunity, cultural pluralism, respect for cultural and lifestyle differences, and support of power equity among groups in the school. The general curriculum for all students is organized around the contribution and perspectives of various cultural groups and utilizes the students' experiential backgrounds and learning styles in promoting bilingualism and multilingualism, and critical analyses of alternative viewpoints. Teachers actively involve students in thinking and analyzing through the use of cooperative learning and other instructional strategies. A diversity focus is evident in classroom decorations, support services, involvement of parents and community members, school menus, library materials, staffing patterns, extracurricular activities, and accessibility of the building.[7]

The approach favored by Sleeter and Grant is **education that is multicultural and social reconstructionist**. They wish to promote social structural equality and cultural pluralism in the society by preparing citizens to work actively toward these goals through education. Therefore, all school children should be taught by a curriculum organized around current social issues involving racism, classism, sexism, and handicapism. They advocate the organization of concepts around experiences and perspectives of several different American groups; use students' life experiences as starting points for analyzing oppression; teach critical thinking skills, analysis of alternative viewpoints, and social action and empowerment skills. They suggest that students should be actively involved in democratic decision-making; instruction should accommodate to diverse learning styles and skill levels through cooperative learning; social action themes should dominate the classroom; testing and grouping which designates some students as failures should be avoided; respect for cultural diversity should be the focus of the school's staffing patterns, school menus, library materials, extra curricular activities, building accessibility, discipline procedures, and support services; and involvement of students, parents, and community members in democratic decision-making about substantive school-wide concerns.[8]

A theoretical framework developed by Milton M. Gordon[9] will also be useful in this task. Gordon did not develop this framework for analyzing multicultural education per se, but rather as a general theory of racial and ethnic group relations and assimilation. Among the constructs he developed or adapted that are especially useful include the three ideological systems for viewing assimilation, "anglo-conformity," the "melting pot," and "cultural pluralism." Gordon writes:

> ...the "anglo-conformity" theory demanded the complete renunciation of the immigrant's ancestral culture in favor of the behavior and values of the Anglo-Saxon core group; the "melting pot" idea envisaged a biological merger of the Anglo-Saxon peoples with other immigrant groups and a blending of their respective cultures into a new indigenous American type; and "cultural pluralism" postulated the preservation of the communal life and significant portions of the culture of the later immigrant groups within the context of American citizenship and political and economic integration to American society.[10]

Gordon also invented the construct **ethclass**:

> I propose...that we refer to the subsociety created by the intersection of the vertical stratifications of ethnicity with the horizontal stratifications of social class as the *ethclass*. Thus a person's *ethclass* might be upper-middle class white, Protestant, or lower-middle class white Irish Catholic, or upper-lower class Negro Protestant, and so on...differences of social class are more important and decisive than differences of ethnic group.[11]

Gordon felt that the major key to the understanding of the ethnic makeup of American society was **structural pluralism**. That is, we are a society largely segregated along ethclass lines, with the dominant factor in terms of behaviors, attitudes, and values being social class. Ethnicity is the subordinate, though still influential, variable. Gordon wrote, "...structural assimilation in substantial fashion has not taken place in America."[12]

Gordon, further, postulated four types of societies with regard to ethnic orientation: racist, assimilationist, **liberal pluralist**, and **corporate pluralist**. The latter two terms will be defined in the text of the analysis.

Anglo-Conformist Educational Policy

The anglo-conformist orientation retains an ascendant position in many school districts and university campuses. Sleeter and Grant's *business as usual, teaching the exceptional and culturally different*, and *human relations* approaches to schooling are anglo-conformist positions. The current debate over so called "political correctness" and/or "multiculturalism" in academe which has been reported in such media as *Newsweek, The New Republic, The New York Times*, and *The Chronicle of Higher Education* is a case in point. A ninety-minute broadcast on National Public Television was devoted to this issue in 1991[13], and others have followed. Essentially the argument of the anti-"political correctness" forces is that a left-wing fascism has taken hold on many campuses in the United States which undermines academic freedom and the free flow of ideas. Professors, and students as well, the argument goes, come under microscopic scrutiny and vicious attack if any fringe political, social, religious, lifestyle or other group conjure up a notion that a sexist, racist, ethnically, behaviorally, or otherwise offensive written statement, remark, joke, innuendo, facial expression, or body language has been directed their way. It is claimed that as "political correctness" has become a semi-official doctrine on these campuses, the academic careers of offending parties are jeopardized and full discussion of alternatives to semi-official policy is restricted or eliminated. Such stalwart defenders of academic freedom as former President George Bush, Boston University's President John Silber[14], The University of Chicago's Allan Bloom[15], the University of Virginia's E. D. Hirsch, Jr.[16], former Secretary of Education and Director of Drug Control Policy William Bennett[17], former Director of The National Endowment for the Humanities Lynne Cheney[18], Dinesh D'Souza[19], and others, are all concerned about this move toward "political correctness."

The curricular dimension of "political correctness," from the point of view of these forces, is a plethora of courses and teaching methodologies which pander to fringe groups and a watering down of the content of mainstream courses. They believe that there is a common core of subject matter which should touch the minds of all students in schools, colleges, and universities, irrespective of sex, ethnic heritage, or social class. Also, there are transcendent truths, great thoughts, great literature, and a line of thinking which bind us together as a nation with a common culture. However, academic standards are undermined and a nation is at risk as a result of this movement toward "political correctness." The curricula of schools, colleges, and universities give short shrift to the great books and great works of mankind, to the ideas and values which have stood the test of time, to the thinkers and leaders in all walks of life who have helped shape the very foundation upon which our national culture rests. Additionally, teachers who are not fully grounded in this traditional subject matter use undemanding methodologies lacking in the rigor to fully develop the rational capacities of students.

This threat to the natural order has been met with an anglo-conformist reform agenda. The *A Nation At Risk* report and *America* (or *Goals*) *2000* are cases in point. They advocate a core curriculum of basic subjects for all students that is intrinsically superior for developing intellectual discipline and through which the values and modes of thinking and behaving of the American core culture are transmitted. They want a longer school day and year, and more homework, so that additional time may be spent on inculcating these truths as well as ratiocination. They feel that teacher training should emphasize specialization in these core subject matters and deemphasize teaching methodologies. They push for a national standardized testing program to measure student progress in these subject matter areas, assess teacher and school accountability, and provide data for comparing our students with those of other countries. They stress the mastery of the basic disciplines through systematic, organized presentation of information, memorization, recitation, and teacher led discussions. It is suggested that these reforms will help us in developing disciplined, intelligent, culturally literate, civilized individuals who share our national values and will work hard to maintain our premier positions in the global economy and military preparedness.

Correlated to these educational policies are contemporary social policy suggestions which call for the restriction of immigration from third world countries (until those already here have a greater period of time to assimilate into the American mainstream culture) and policies making English the official national language.

Culturally Pluralistic Educational Policy

Even if immigration and language restrictions are put in place, the present demographic shifts to a minority-majority places the anglo-conformist position in jeopardy, in spite of it being the **power elite**'s policy formulation of choice. Instead, ever since 1915, when Horace M. Kallen[20] began calling for a culturally pluralistic interpretation of the United States, voices have been raised favoring an educational orientation which reflects that interpretation. In 1916 John Dewey called for a study of America's various heritages in the public schools.[21] The *intercultural education* movement of the 1940s and 1950s attempted to reconcile the right of diverse groups to maintain their identities with the responsibilities of democratic citizenship by affording individuals the option of being either "ethnic" or not, as they might see fit.[22] The Civil Rights Movement of the 1960s gave further impetus to the idea of education that was multicultural.

Many authors have written with eloquence and passion from this frame of reference. Over the past twenty years, James A. Banks has developed and refined his conceptions of multicultural education.[23] Other academicians have also participated in the ongoing conversation about multicultural education in theoretical and hypothetical terms.[24] Banks sees multicultural education as "an idea or concept, an educational reform movement, and a process."[25] Among the transformative aspects of multicultural education from this point of view is an ethnic studies curriculum for all students, infused throughout their educational experience.[26] A basic goal shared by the multiculturalists is educational and social equity.

Two educational policy positions emanating from a culturally pluralistic interpretation of American ideals and realities have emerged in the 1990s. The first owes some allegiance to the aforementioned *intercultural education* movement and can best be termed *liberally pluralistic*. Milton Gordon defines *liberal pluralism* as:

> ...the absence, even prohibition, of any legal or governmental recognition of racial, religious, language, or national origins...and a prohibition of the use of ethnic criteria of any type for discriminatory purposes, or conversely for special or favored treatment...Equalitarian norms in such a society would emphasize equality of opportunity and evaluation of individuals on the basis of universalistic standards of performance. Structural pluralism...would exist voluntarily...as would cultural pluralism, at the will of the ethnic group members.[27]

The goals of a liberally pluralistic multicultural education are panhumanistic, **metacultural**, and liberating.[28] Sleeter and Grant's conception designated as *multicultural education* may be subsumed by this construct. By coming to grips with his or her ethnicity and the ethnicity of others and gaining the conceptual wherewithal for critical, reflective, open, flexible, sharable inquiry into the contexts through which humans interpret their worlds, the learner escapes ethnic encapsulation. The person is, thereby, equipped for citizenship in a complex, rapidly changing, socio-economically stratified and structurally pluralistic, multicultural, multiracial society characterized by a multiplicity of segmented value orientations but which, at least nominally, espouses democracy as its way of life. Through an integrated and multidisciplinary, multicultural curriculum touching all subject matters and all grade levels, alternative cultural contexts for reality and value formation and knowledge construction are explored and problems confronted. In this way, problem solving ability and commitments to open and ongoing inquiry into and reconstruction of values are cultivated. An amendable system of judgment is developed which tests proposed solutions to problems, and ideas in general, on the basis of their probable consequences for human social growth, welfare, and development in a multicultural society and world. The curriculum is inquiry, rather than subject matter, centered. All areas of investigations are approached through a multicultural prism. The contributions, sensitivities, and analytic contexts of the diverse groups which make up our society and world are taken into account and the frames of reference of a variety of subject matters (their models, methods, and theorems) are utilized in the conduct of the inquiry. The teacher in this type of multicultural education is much more than a subject matter specialist. Teachers are co-inquirers who, taking into account and accommodating to differences in student learning and language styles, values, attitudes, and beliefs, serve as facilitators, arrangers of experiences, and research project directors.[29] The ideal setting for this kind of inquiry involves a school desegregated across ethclass lines which is truly multicultural and socioeconomically heterogeneous. Issues of concern to students from different ethclass groups could, thereby, be more easily shared in heterogeneously grouped classes and alternative cultural contexts explored in collaborative problem solving. The cultural orientations, learning, and language styles of the various ethclass groups would be respected. For example, both Western and non-Western world views and the learning styles of diverse and traditional students can be accommodated.[30]

In order to facilitate cross-cultural communication, understanding, and collaborative problem solving, a liberally pluralistic education would include programs of bilingual and bidialectal education. Standard English would be taught to speakers of non-standard English, and languages other than English, in such a way that the home language was neither denigrated nor replaced. Languages and dialects other than standard English would be taught to the English speakers as well. Liberal pluralists claim that, while respecting diversity, this approach prepares students for full participation in a society which espouses democratic, egalitarian, pluralistic ideals.

Educational materials which reflect the cultural diversity of the nation and world, their histories, literatures, religions, myths, legends, and conceptual orientations would get full play in a liberally pluralistic education.

Other practices favored by the liberal pluralists include cooperative learning, whole language approaches, human relations training for teachers, community involvement in school policy decisions, inservice teacher training in multicultural education, student involvement in curriculum planning and other policy decisions, and an inter-racial student council.

There is a second multicultural education policy formulation which also views the United States as a culturally pluralistic society, but which favors a *corporately pluralistic* orientation toward ethnicity. Milton Gordon writes that "corporate pluralism" refers to a social situation in which:

> ...racial and ethnic groups are formally recognized as legally constituted entities with official standing in the society. Economic and political rewards...are allocated on the basis of numerical quotas...Equalitarian emphasis is on equality of condition rather than equality of opportunity...cultural pluralism tends to be reinforced...structural pluralism is officially encouraged.[31]

Corporate pluralists see the issues of culture and ethnicity primarily in terms of power imbalances where dominant groups exploit and oppress subordinate groups. They favor a multicultural education which sensitizes majority group children to cultures different from their own and engages children of subordinate groups in critical analyses of their own condition.

The students are, thereby, conceptually equipped with the means of resisting the oppression of the dominant group. Empowerment of subordinate groups to overcome the "tyranny of the majority" is a major focus of the corporate pluralists. The ultimate goal of a corporately pluralistic multicultural education is to create a new world order in which formerly oppressed groups are in control of their own destinies. Multicultural and global education are inextricably bound because injustice and oppression are global phenomena. The school must expose inequities and play a pivotal role in righting the social imbalances that produce gaps between rich and poor groups and nations; racial, religious, and gender discrimination; and other invidious social distinctions.[32] The social activist aspects of Sleeter and Grant's designation *education that is multicultural and social reconstructionist* can be seen here.

Those advocating *single-group studies* sometimes take this a step beyond the social reconstructionists by advocating that it is important for minority ethnic groups to maintain their cultural traditions, languages, and group solidarity. From this point of view, multicultural education means cultural maintenance through a curriculum composed of courses on specific ethnic groups, taught by ethnic group members. Ethnic minority members are taught by role models who share their ethnic experience.

These teachers serve as educational statespersons and social activists who engage students in critical inquiry into social problems affecting their groups and in devising strategies for planned change in contemporary society. Students examine the national and world situation through the prism of their group's ethnic experience. Afrocentric, hispanocentric, and other **ethnocentric** points of view serve the purposes of providing students with pride in their own heritages and mechanisms for critical analyses of the national culture. In this way, vehicles for penetrating the national power structure may be developed. Students are encouraged to question the status quo, investigate controversial issues, develop alternatives, and work in society to put these alternatives into practice.

The recent attempts by Spencer Holland, Director of the Center for the Education of African American Males at Morgan State University, and others to institute African American Male Academies in Baltimore and Detroit, in which African American male children are taught by African American male teachers, are illustrations of this approach, although advocates for the separate classes and schools for African

American males are concerned as much with sheer survival in American culture as they are with cultural maintenance.[33]

DESCRIPTIONS OF MULTICULTURAL EDUCATION

Have the past twenty years of theoretical development in multicultural education had significant impact on actual school practices? A series of studies conducted between 1974 and 1980 offer descriptions of multicultural education in public schools, colleges, and universities during these years.[34]

Public Schools

Washburn's 1974 survey of the 720 largest public school districts in the United States, briefly mentioned in the first chapter, showed that many of the nation's large public school districts were attempting to enhance cross-cultural understanding through multicultural education. The survey, answered by over 55% (397) of all U.S. school districts with more than 10,000 students, revealed that 72.5% had introduced ethnic studies into their academic curricula.

Of the districts responding, 14.6% included data from elementary schools only, 20.7% from secondary schools only, and 64.7% from both elementary and secondary schools. The "average" school district reported a European American student population of 61% to 70%, with the median at 81% to 90% European American.

Most of the school districts which reported ethnic studies curricula stated that their programs were less than four years old. Over 66% of the districts reporting included human relations training for teachers in an effort to enhance teachers' understanding of themselves and sensitize them to the needs and feelings of others. Almost half of the 397 school districts responding to the questionnaire included inservice training in multicultural education to better prepare teachers to reach students whose cultural backgrounds differed from their own, as well as to teach intelligently about the varying cultures in the United States.

The responses of the 288 school districts which reported having ethnic studies in their curricula were compared with the 109 which did not. In each case, a higher proportion of those schools having ethnic studies curricula utilized other practices to create cross-cultural understanding or to form closer links between school and community. It appeared that the inclusion of the study of ethnic groups in the academic program denoted a broader commitment to inter-ethnic and general human understanding.

No appreciable differences were noted in the ethnic composition of the faculties in districts possessing ethnic studies and those which had no such programs. The districts reporting ethnic studies curricula had, on the average, slightly higher proportions of African American, Hispanic American, Native American, and other cultural groups, and a lower proportion of European Americans among their student populations.

Seventy-four percent of those districts reporting ethnic studies curricula had instituted human relations training for teachers, as opposed to 47.7% of those with no ethnic studies curricula. Similarly, 69.8% of the districts with ethnic studies curricula reported community involvement in school policy decisions, while only 39.4% of the 109 districts without ethnic studies curricula claimed community involvement in decision-making.

Other differences between the two types of school districts were:
- a strong school/community public relations program: districts with ethnic studies programs, 58%; districts without ethnic studies, 39.4%;
- inservice teacher training in multicultural education: 56.6% versus 30.3%;
- student involvement in curriculum planning: 53.1% versus 22.9%;
- a multicultural curriculum: 42.4% versus 19.3%;
- a community-centered instructional program: 30.6% versus 16.5%.

The study revealed that the districts reporting ethnic studies curricula tended to be more deeply involved in multicultural education than those districts which had no such curricula. However, the 288 districts which appeared to have made a marked attempt at multicultural education represented only 40% of the total 720 school districts with more than 10,000 students. The author concluded that between 1969 and 1974 the increasing inclusion of ethnic studies curricula marked a major step in the direction of cross-cultural understanding. Assimilation models in education, through which all children are expected to blend into the "mainstream," were beginning to be replaced by those which more nearly reflected the reality of our culturally pluralistic society—that there was no one model American.

The 288 school districts (40%) reporting an ethnic studies curriculum in 1974 had not had them long. Nearly 82% of the programs had been in operation for five years or less, with the average at slightly under four years. This corresponded to the 4.2% which had been engaged in ethnic studies for ten years or more.

The number of students per district participating in the ethnic studies programs showed great variation. Ten and one-half percent of the districts had fewer than 100 students involved, while 19.4% had more than 10,000 participating. The average number of students per district engaged in ethnic studies was 3,370, although the median figure (950) was considerably lower.

A large proportion (80.9%) reported community involvement of some type in their ethnic studies programs. The types of community involvement included: the use of community resources (74.7%); the use of human resources in the community (69.8%); interaction with community organizations (55.2%); community involvement in curriculum planning (41.4%); study of the community (40.3%); and a community based instructional program (16%).

African Americans were the most widely studied cultural group in school districts reporting ethnic studies programs. Ninety-two percent of these districts included African Americans in their ethnic studies curricula. The next two most widely studied groups were Mexican Americans (70.5%) and Native Americans (67%).

Ethnic studies in the public school districts of the United States having student populations of 10,000 or more most often concerned themselves with the history of the cultural group studied. While 94.8% included history in their ethnic studies curricula, 82.6% delved into social customs, and 71.5% examined the relationships between culture and personality.

The results of this survey revealed that the major growth in the adoption of ethnic studies curricula among schools serving student populations of 10,000 or more had occurred since 1969. The bulk of these programs was begun between 1969 and 1972, with fewer programs being initiated in the following two years. With only 40% of the 720 school districts reporting ethnic studies curricula, it was unclear if these declining figures represented a trend.

The author concluded that in only a small proportion of the districts queried were all or most of the student populations touched by ethnic studies. If we were to gain an understanding of the ways of living of the peoples who populate our land and come to appreciate the contributions made by each of these groups, a broader proportion of our students should have come into contact with information and experiences pertaining to our diverse cultures.

It appeared that among our largest school districts a core of concern for inter-ethnic understanding existed, as exemplified by the inclusion of ethnic studies in their curricula. Some seemed to be committed to the inclusion of a broad scope of the peoples of the United States in their programs. Many districts afforded students the opportunity to deal with the historical and sociocultural issues involved. The tragedy was that the core of concern represented an apparent minority of the school districts serving student populations of 10,000 or more and that these programs had been so long in coming.

By 1977, the Commonwealth of Pennsylvania, through legislation and Department of Education regulations, had made a commitment to multiethnic education at all levels.

In an effort to determine if this state-level commitment actually reached the local school district, the Multicultural Education Center of Bloomsburg (Pa.) State College surveyed Pennsylvania's 504 public school systems, twenty-nine intermediate units, and fifty-six vocational-technical schools. Responses to questionnaires were received from 483 public school systems (95.8%), forty-six vocational-technical schools (82.1%), and all intermediate units. Of the 589 elements of public education (K-12) within Pennsylvania, 558 completed questionnaires— a 94.7% rate of return. Of these 558 respondents, 129 (24.4%) reported having ethnic studies programs.

African Americans were the most widely studied group among the 129 systems reporting ethnic studies programs; 110 (85.3%) of these school systems studied African Americans. Native Americans were studied in ninety-one cases (70.5%), while German Americans and Japanese Americans were studied in sixty-five school systems (50.4%). In all, seventy-four ethnic groups were studied in Pennsylvania's public schools.

These studies were accomplished through 3,219 units of study, 539 courses, and 136 curricula. Two hundred eighty-five of the units of study dealt with African Americans (8.9%), 199 with Native Americans (6.2%), 123 with Chinese Americans (3.8%), 119 with Jewish Americans (3.7%), 109 with Amish (3.4%), and 107 with Japanese Americans (3.3%). Of the courses, African Americans (13.7%) and Native Americans (8.9%) lead the list with seventy-four and forty-eight, respectively. There were twelve African American studies curricula (8.8%) and ten on Native Americans (7.4%), but the largest single type of curriculum was multiethnic (sixteen, or 11.8%). Of these units, courses, and curricula, 141 dealt exclusively with the Pennsylvania ethnic experience, and 811 had portions that focused on the experiences of ethnic groups in the Commonwealth.

Most of the programs were of recent origin. Only one school system had been offering ethnic studies for more than ten years. The average number of years of operation was 4.2, with the median being 3.5 years. Thirty of the programs had been under way for two years or less.

The heaviest concentration of ethnic studies was found in the last two years of high school. Ninety-seven schools (75.2%) provided ethnic studies in the eleventh and twelfth grades. In Pennsylvania as a whole, all grade levels were included, with fifteen schools having such programs in kindergarten (11.6%). The number of schools offering ethnic studies at each grade level increased rather steadily through the ninth grade, at which point fifty-three schools (41%) offered such studies.

In all, more than 84,464 public school students in the Commonwealth of Pennsylvania were involved in ethnic studies each year. Twelve systems (9.3%) enrolled more than 2,000 pupils per year, whereas thirty-six systems (27.9%) had fewer than 100 students involved in ethnic studies.

The students most often studied ethnic history, with 119 schools (92.2%) focusing on that aspect. Social customs (110 schools, 85.3%), culture and personality (107 schools, 82.9%), religion (101 schools, 78.3%), attitudes (ninety-eight schools, 76%), and values (ninety-four schools, 72.9%), were other cultural elements frequently studied.

A wide variety of social science concepts were utilized by the Commonwealth's public school systems in their ethnic studies programs. The anthropological concepts of culture (117 schools, 90.7%) and race (108 schools, 83.7%) occurred most frequently. Prejudice (108 schools, 83.7%), discrimination (106 schools, 82.2%), and racism (99 schools, 76.7%) were sociological concepts that guided inquiry into the ethnic experience. From economics, poverty (103 schools, 79.8%), and from the discipline of history, immigration (ninety-nine schools, 76.7%) were used to expand students' frameworks for understanding ethnicity. The ghetto as a geographical concept appeared in many programs (ninety-six schools, 74.4%).

Folklore, too, played a part in some of Pennsylvania's 129 systems that offered ethnic studies programs. Folk customs were explored by ninety-five of the districts (73.6%), as were legends (49.6%), superstitions (48.1%), folk music (45%), and other oral, non-oral, and material culture traditions.

Seventy of the systems (54.3%) had some type of community involvement in ethnic studies. Sixty-four of them (91.4%) used members of the community as resource people, whereas fifty-five used other community resources (78.5%). Forty systems (57.1%) studied ethnicity in their local communities; twenty-nine (41.4%) interacted with community organizations in an effort to enrich the students' ethnic studies experiences.

Although ethnic studies at the school district level had not reached the level of commitment expressed by the Pennsylvania Department of Education, growth was evident. Most of the programs were new. However, since only 24% of the systems reported having ethnic studies, in a sense all the Commonwealth's ethnic groups were under-represented in curricula. For instance, Slavic groups represented 28% of Pennsylvania's population, but aside from Russians (fifty school systems), no Slavic peoples were represented in more than twenty-seven ethnic studies programs. Italians, 17% of the Commonwealth's population, fared a little better (fifty-five school systems), and Germans (15% of the population) appeared in the programs of sixty-five school systems.

Teacher Education

These studies indicated that multiethnic and multicultural studies were fast becoming regular features of United States public education. As these programs grew in number and importance, the need increased for well-trained personnel to teach in them.

In 1978, in order to find out how higher education was responding to this need, Washburn surveyed 3,038 postsecondary institutions in the United States, its territories, and possessions. His first aim was to identify institutions that offered a major, a minor, or a concentration in either bilingual/bicultural or multicultural education. Of the 2,542 institutions (85%) whose officials responded, 241 said that their institutions offered bilingual/bicultural teacher education programs and 135 reported that their institutions offered multicultural programs. He then mailed questionnaires to these institutions. Representatives of 226 (94%) of the bilingual/bicultural programs and 120 (84%) of the multicultural programs completed and returned these questionnaires.

The multicultural teacher education programs served more than 23,332 students in a total of 1,996 courses that focused on 38 ethnic groups. In addition, ninety-four of the schools (78.3%) provided a total of 587 general or theoretical multicultural education courses, and ninety-two schools (76.7%) offered a total of 377 courses on methods and materials for multicultural education. Student teaching (ninety-six schools, 80%), practicums (seventy-eight schools, 65%), and/or internships (fifty-eight schools, 48.3%) were offered in cross-cultural settings.

The bilingual/bicultural programs served more than 43,378 students with a total of 4,197 courses that focused on forty-two ethnic groups. Forty different languages were taught. In addition, 184 of the schools (81.4%) offered a total of 1,210 general or theoretical courses that provided conceptual orientations to bilingual/bicultural education, and 180 schools (79.7%) offered a total of 864 courses dealing with methods or materials for bilingual/bicultural education. For practical experience, 142 schools (62.8%) offered student teaching, 138 (61.1%) offered practicums, and eighty-eight (38.9%) offered internships in bilingual settings.

Thirty-five schools offered undergraduate multicultural education majors; thirty offered minors. At the graduate level, twenty schools offered majors and fourteen offered minors. Twenty-four schools offered master's degrees with a concentration in multicultural education, and seven schools had doctoral programs. The average program was less than seven years old and served 201 students.

Undergraduate bilingual/bicultural majors were offered by seventy-four schools; sixty offered minors. There were thirty-seven schools offering graduate majors and twenty-seven with minors. Twenty-one schools awarded associate's degrees, seventy-four awarded bachelor's degrees, seventy-four awarded master's degrees, and ten awarded doctoral degrees. The average program was seven years old and served 228 students.

Twenty-five different academic disciplines participated in the multicultural teacher education programs. Those most frequently involved included: education (109 schools, 90.8%), history (seventy-seven schools, 64.2%), sociology (seventy-six schools, 63.3%), anthropology (sixty-seven schools, 55.8%), foreign languages (fifty-nine schools, 49.2%), linguistics (fifty-four schools, 45%), and political science (fifty-two schools, 43.3%). Those disciplines most frequently involved in bilingual/bicultural programs include: education (179 schools, 78.9%), foreign languages (172 schools, 75.8%), history (150 schools, 66.1%), sociology (137 schools, 60.4%), linguistics (119 schools, 52.4%), anthropology (116 schools, 51.1%), and English (110 schools, 48.5%).

Community involvement was an important feature of both multicultural (85%) and bilingual/bicultural (81.9%) teacher education programs. Many schools made use of community resources—especially human resources—in developing their programs. Others interacted with community organizations, studying the community itself, or involved community members in curriculum planning.

Postsecondary institutions with multicultural teacher education programs were found in thirty-three states and the District of Columbia. California had the largest number (twenty-six). Pennsylvania and Texas (eight schools each), Massachusetts and New York (six schools each), and Illinois and Wisconsin (five schools each) followed.

Bilingual/bicultural programs were offered by institutions in thirty-three states, the District of Columbia, Guam, and the Virgin Islands. California had fifty-nine schools with such programs; Texas was next with twenty-four, followed by New York (twenty-two), Illinois (fourteen), and Pennsylvania (eleven).

Although sixteen of the schools offering multicultural teacher education identified their programs as multiethnic in nature, the heaviest emphasis overall was on Hispanic American, African American, Asian American, and Native American groups. Of 1,996 courses that focused on specific groups, 692 (34.7%) concentrated on Hispanic Americans. There were 424 courses (21.2%) on African Americans, 204 (10.2%) on Asian Americans, and 178 courses (8.9%) on Native Americans.

The overwhelming majority of the bilingual/bicultural programs (80.1%) focused on the Spanish language. The study of Hispanic cultures also predominated. Of the 209 schools that offered courses on the experiences of specific groups in the United States, 116 (55.5%) offered a total of 1,126 courses (26.8% of all such courses offered) on Mexican Americans. Fifty-one schools (24.4%) offered 350 courses on Puerto Ricans; forty-four (21.1%) offered 256 courses on Spanish Americans; twenty-five (12%) offered 109 courses on Cuban Americans; twenty-two (10.5%) offered seventy-four courses on South Americans; and nineteen (9.1%) offered seventy courses on Central Americans.

Among the thirty-nine other languages taught in bilingual/bicultural programs were: Italian (fourteen schools), French (ten schools), and Native American languages (ten schools). The Native American languages were Cherokee, Choctaw, Cree, Eskimo, Navajo, Seminole/ Creek, and Tlingit. Among the nineteen schools (8.4%) that taught Asian languages, Cantonese, Chinese, Vietnamese, Japanese, and Korean were offered. Two schools taught Franco-Haitian. Three provided Swahili and one, Yiddish.

The forty-two cultural groups studied in these programs included African Americans (by sixty-one schools in 514 courses), Native Americans (by fifty-one schools in 315 courses), Chinese Americans (by eighteen schools in sixty-three courses), and Japanese Americans (by fourteen schools in thirty-three courses).

The findings revealed that schools offering multicultural and/or bilingual/bicultural teacher education provided students with a balance of theory, methods, and information on specific groups. They also provided a fair degree of actual cross-cultural contact through student teaching, internships, and practicums. Research indicated that direct, cross-cultural contact had the most dramatic impact on trainee attitudes and behavior.[35]

These programs were recent developments at the time, and they tended to stress large and visible minority groups. Other groups, most notably those with central-, eastern-, or southern-European heritages, had not been well represented. In addition, very few schools offered fully developed programs, and only a small number of prospective teachers were touched by broadly based, multidisciplinary curricula that contained experiential components. Even fewer were able to take advantage of advanced academic programs.

Ethnic Studies in Higher Education

In 1978, cultural pluralism as a guiding factor in curriculum building at higher educational institutions in the United States appeared to be a recent phenomenon as well.[36] In 1975, Richard Gambino reported that 135 colleges and universities offered ethnic studies courses or programs. These programs took three principle forms: those which focused on one ethnic group; departmental programs; and programs in which ethnic studies were made an integral part of the standard courses offered.[37]

McConville's 1975 study[38] of higher education institutions in the southwest revealed nearly 100 ethnic studies programs, whereas Bengelsdorf's 1972 work[39] reported that at that time there were courses or programs being offered on Asian Americans (forty-three schools), African Americans (266 schools with courses, forty-one programs, sixty-nine degrees), Chicanos (104 schools), Native Americans (forty-two schools with courses, eight degrees), Puerto Ricans (fourteen schools, Finnish Americans (one school), French Americans (six schools), Jewish Americans (180 undergraduate and twenty-five advanced degree programs), Polish Americans (fifty-five programs), Portuguese Americans (one school), and thirty-eight schools which offered multiethnic courses (four major/minors, three degrees).

In some quarters ethnic studies was equated with minority studies[40], whereas others called for broadly conceptualized comparative, interdisciplinary or multidisciplinary, multiethnic approaches in the development of ethnic studies programs.[41] Pierre L. van den Berghe warned that:

> Ethnic studies as an adjunct of politically organized ethnic groups must almost inevitably result in extreme intellectual parochialism. Motivated by an ideology that extols the "unique" experience of each group, and glorifying the study of each group in isolation and for its own sake, ethnic studies condemn themselves to an inability to understand the nature of *inter*-group relations.[42]

Although Gambino wrote that, "Well conceived programs of ethnic studies would invite people of all ethnic backgrounds to participate at all stages of scholarship and teaching, subject solely to their qualifications as scholars, teachers or students,"[43] in their study of the articulation between ethnic studies and affirmative action, Record and Record (1974) found that in minority studies programs "...race or ethnicity, long denounced as a criterion, was elevated to primary importance as a requisite for employment,"[44] and non-academic, political criteria were used for hiring as well as maintenance of employment. They stated further that "...affirmative action issued from the equalitarian-integrationist-universalist tradition of the liberal establishment [whereas]...the new minority studies programs [especially Black studies]...inevitably assumed a strongly *separatist* bent."[45]

However, among those who had published suggestions for the structure and content of higher education ethnic studies programs, the majority favored a conceptual, comparative approach which recognized the social, cultural, political, and economic complexities of a culturally pluralistic urban, industrial society as well as the organic nature of ethnic groups, their internal diversity and stratification.[46] A number also felt that student involvement in ethnic communities and community involvement in program development would have been welcomed features of an ethnic studies program.[47]

In light of these analyses of and suggestions for higher education ethnic studies programs, and in an effort to determine the *state of the art* of ethnic studies, 3,038 postsecondary institutions in the United States and outlying areas were surveyed during the 1977-78 academic year. Of the 3,038 schools queried, 2,536 responses were received, six schools were reported to have closed, and 496 did not reply. The rate of response from the 3,038 schools, less the six no longer operating, was 84%. Five hundred twenty-six schools reported that they had ethnic studies programs. Responses were received from 439 schools (84%) with ethnic studies programs.

The 439 schools provided over 99,200 students a total of 8,805 courses on sixty-two ethnic groups, 316 undergraduate majors, 283 undergraduate minors, fifty-eight graduate majors, thirty-one graduate minors, ninety-four associate's degrees, 240 bachelor's degrees, eighty-five master's degrees, twenty doctoral degrees, and 159 certificates. Two hundred seventy-nine (64%) of these schools offered a total of 1,818 general or theoretical courses which did not focus on particular groups as such, but which furnished conceptual orientations to ethnicity. One hundred ninety-five of them (44%) had a total of 812 courses which dealt with methods and/or materials for teaching and/or working across cultures. In addition, 105 of these schools (24%) offered student teaching, 135 (31%) had practica, and 113 (26%) featured internships in settings which provided for cross -cultural contact.

The average program had been in operation for seven years and served 342 students. The disciplines most frequently involved in higher education ethnic studies programs were history (375 schools, 85%), sociology (329 schools, 75%), political science (261 schools, 59%), English (240 schools, 55%), and anthropology (237 schools, 54%).

The schools with ethnic studies programs were located in forty-eight states and the District of Columbia, with the largest numbers in California (ninety-six schools, 22%), New York (forty-five schools, 10%), Ohio (twenty-three schools, 5%), Pennsylvania (twenty-one schools, 4.8%), and Washington (twenty schools, 4.6%). By region, the Middle Atlantic, that portion of the Middle West east of the Mississippi River, and the far west, housed the bulk of the programs. A large proportion (341 schools, 78%) reported community involvement of some type in their programs. The types of community involvement included: the use of human resources in the community (262 schools, 60%), use of community resources (256 schools, 58%), interaction with community organizations (252 schools, 57%), study of the community (182 schools, 41%), community involvement in curriculum planning (ninety-three schools, 21%), and a community based instructional program (sixty-eight schools, 15%). As well, 172 schools (39%) had produced materials for use in their programs. Many of these materials were available for loan or purchase.

The heaviest emphasis in ethnic studies programs in the United States was upon African American, Hispanic American, Native American, and Asian American groups. Many more programs and courses dealt with these groups and, by far, the largest number of students participated in these programs. There were 7,343 courses (83% of the total) which focused on the United States' experiences of these groups. In contrast there were 787 courses (9% of the total) which focused on European American groups. The same pattern held true in courses and programs which purported to be multiethnic in nature. Functionally then, ethnic studies programs in the institutions of higher education in the United States were, by and large, minority studies programs. The equation of ethnic studies with minority studies in a portion of the ethnic studies literature was somewhat understandable in light of this fact. It was much more probable that the non-academic public would be likely to have a similar perception as well.

Most programs focused on a single ethnic group, although there were a large number of courses designed to provide conceptual orientations to ethnicity being offered. There was a wide range of multidisciplinary involvement in these programs. There was a substantial amount of community involvement in the programs as well.

The development of ethnic studies programs was largely a phenomenon of the 1970s, the bulk of the programs appearing between 1968 and 1976. Programs dealing with European American ethnic groups had been in operation for a somewhat longer duration (an average of 7.3 years) than others, with those focusing on Slavic American groups being the oldest (7.5 year average). African American studies (6.4 years), Asian

American studies (6.5 years), and programs focusing on Hispanic American groups (6.3 years) had, on the average, been in operation for about the same period of time. Native American studies programs were of slightly more recent vintage (5.3 years). Groups whose programs had been underway for the shortest period of time included Arab Americans (4.5 years), Greek Americans (4.4 years), and Irish Americans (4.6 years).

The author concluded that an argument had been made that the general curricula of institutions of higher education in the United States had for so long reflected the Anglo-Teutonic tradition, that groups, especially those which had suffered invidious distinctions, must have separate programs controlled and taught by representatives of those groups; that, in the absence of this kind of power base, the heritage, perceptions, sensibilities, contributions, and experiences of the non-WASP peoples would receive short shrift and most likely, would be bastardized in the process. This was, of course, a political, rather than academic argument. The political argument may have been valid. The academic validity of courses and programs so constructed, however, should have been more closely scrutinized, especially in regard to propensities toward ethnic chauvinism and intellectual parochialism.

This survey indicated that during that period of time certain groups had been successful in gaining a place in curricula at a small number of the country's postsecondary institutions which served, relatively speaking, a small student population. In light of our nations's history, others, most notably central-, eastern-, and southern-European heritage groups appeared to be under-represented.

If the nation's schools were to adequately prepare citizens for responsible participation in a complex, culturally pluralistic society and a multicultural world, the general education which college students received should have reflected the realities of that society and world. That would have entailed the development of broadly based, conceptually oriented, multidisciplinary, comparative, multiethnic curricula to have been a part of the education of each college or university student. Further, the standard for professorship in all programs, multiethnic or focused on single groups, should have been scholarly merit.

In 1978 there were over two thousand postsecondary institutions in the United States with no ethnic studies programs. To the extent that these schools did not provide their students with a pluralistic view of life within the United States and beyond in their general education curricula, and to the extent they maintained an ontological commitment to an Anglo-

Teutonic perception of the world, they were agents for the perpetuation of "cultural deprivation."

National and State Policies

Donna M. Gollnick has updated the study of national and state policies on multicultural education she and Raymond H. Giles conducted in 1977.[48] She found that very little progress had been made in federal legislation on multicultural education with a continued emphasis on equal educational opportunity for ethnic minorities and students with disabilities. The Ethnic Heritage Studies Act (Title IX of the Elementary and Secondary Education Act) which, beginning in 1972, promoted the development of curriculum materials for ethnic studies was eliminated during the early days of the administration of President Ronald Reagan. The minimal amount of federal funding for curriculum materials or models which remained "...focused on the provision of equal educational opportunity for female students, students of color, limited-English proficiency students, students from low-income families, and students with disabilities."[49] Federal desegregation efforts have had little impact, especially on reducing segregation of students *within* schools. In terms of Sleeter and Grant's typology of conceptions of multicultural education, federal initiatives focused on teaching the culturally different and students with disabilities, rather than education that is multicultural.

In 1977 Giles and Gollnick found twenty-eight states which, in one way or another, supported multicultural education. "By 1993, 35 states had regulations or policies related to ethnicity, race, class, gender and/or other cultural groups. Forty states had requirements that schools and/or teacher education include the study of one or more ethnic groups, human relations, cultural diversity, multicultural education, and/or bilingual education."[50] The state regulations or policies run the gamut of Sleeter and Grant's typology. All states responding to Gollnick's survey maintained a focus on *teaching the exceptional and culturally different*. Six states required *single-group studies*. Three states mandated *human relations* training in teacher education. Thirty-three states focused on cultural diversity, but only nineteen used the term *multicultural education*. Fourteen states issued regulations for multicultural curricula, but only four required accountability; and, without legislation requiring monitoring, guidelines tended to be ignored.

As was true in the mid-1970s, many non-governmental agencies and associations were supportive of multicultural education, although their recommendations remained voluntary. The National Council on the Accreditation of Teacher Education continues, through their standards, to require the inclusion of multicultural education in the 500 teacher education programs they accredit. Gollnick states, "...over 80% of the institutions reviewed by NCATE between 1988 and 1993 have incorporated multicultural education into the curriculum at least at a minimal level."[51]

The question remains:

What impact have the conceptual and theoretical developments in the field of multicultural education and national and state initiatives for multicultural education had on the actual practice of public schools in the United States circa 1995?

CHAPTER THREE

The 1995 Multicultural Education Survey

IN ORDER TO MEASURE THE ACTUAL PRACTICE OF MULTICULTURAL EDUCATION in the nation's public school districts, we replicated and updated Washburn's 1974 survey of the 720 districts in the United States which served student populations of 10,000 or more.[1] In 1995 there were 713 such school districts.[2] These districts constituted the population we surveyed during the 1995 calendar year in an attempt to determine the status of multicultural education in the United States.

The purposes of our 1995 study included discovering how many of the 713 school districts had multicultural education programs, and, for those which did, the nature and extent of each program. We wished to compare these data with those gathered by Washburn in 1974. In addition to replicating Washburn's survey, we updated our study so that we could categorize the contemporary practice of multicultural education in the United States according to the typology developed by Sleeter and Grant.[3] In particular we wanted to know: how long each program had been in operation; which grade levels were involved; how many students participated per academic school year; the ethnic composition of the districts' student, administrative, instructional, and support staff populations; the extent and nature of community involvement in the multicultural education programs; the social and school goals of each program; the program's curricular and instructional aims; the aspects of the classroom incorporated into the program; the school practices employed; the materials they had developed for their program; and, whether any locally produced materials were available for purchase. In addition, if one of the school practices employed by the district included an ethnic studies curriculum, our inquiry included the ethnic groups studied; the disciplines participating; and which elements concerning the groups were studied.

Initially a query letter (**APPENDIX A**) was sent to the superintendent of each of the 713 school districts. This letter briefly described the nature and purposes of the project and asked the superintendent to provide information by filling out a form on the reverse side of the letter. This form had *no* and *yes* boxes to be checked depending on whether or not the district had a multicultural education program or programs. If the *yes* box was checked, the superintendent was asked to provide the names, titles, addresses, and phone numbers in spaces provided for program directors or contact persons. In the letter we asked the superintendent to alert those persons to the fact that they would be part of a national study of multicultural education. A postage-paid return envelope was included with the letter.

If no response was received within a few weeks, we sent a follow-up letter with a postage-paid envelope requesting the same information (**APPENDIX B**). For those who did not respond to this second mailing we made phone calls (sometimes as many as five or six) until responses were received from all 713 school districts.

In turn, a cover letter (**APPENDIX C**), the *Multicultural Education Survey* instrument (**APPENDIX D**), and a postage-paid return envelope were sent to the program directors at each of the 329 school districts (46.14% of all school districts serving a student population of 10,000 or more) which indicated that they had multicultural education programs. The same follow-up procedure that was used with the query letter was utilized in an attempt to secure responses to our questionnaire. In this manner returns were received from 255 school districts, a return rate of 77.08%. These data are described on a state by state basis in **TABLES 1 AND 2** and a regional basis in **TABLE 3**.

All questionnaire responses were converted to scantron sheets and computer analyzed using the Statistical Package for the Social Studies (SPSS) program. The descriptive analyses include statistics for all 255 school district multicultural education programs and a contrastive analysis of these data with the results of Washburn's 1974 study. Also investigated comparatively are programs which have ethnic studies curricula and those which do not. These data are also contrasted to the 1974 results.

New to the 1995 research are analyses of the programs, utilizing Sleeter and Grant's typology. Programs with different social goals, school goals, curricular aims, and instructional aims are analyzed in terms of the other variables mentioned above.

These descriptive analyses detailed in the next chapter offer a rather complete picture of the status of public school multicultural education programs in the United States. They provide information for critical evaluation of the contemporary practice of education characterized as multicultural by practitioners and theoreticians alike. We offer our own critique and speculative analysis in our final chapter.

TABLE 1
Multicultural Education Programs by State, 1995

State	School Districts Serving 10,000+ Students N	School Districts with Multicultural Education Programs N	%	School Districts Responding to Survey N	%	School Districts with No Multicultural Education Programs N	%
Alabama	12	3	25.00	3	100.00	9	75.00
Alaska	3	2	66.67	2	100.00	1	33.33
Arizona	18	9	50.00	8	88.89	9	50.00
Arkansas	3	3	100.00	3	100.00	0	0.00
California	128	39	30.47	31	79.49	89	69.53
Colorado	18	9	50.00	7	77.78	9	50.00
Connecticut	5	4	80.00	2	50.00	1	20.00
Delaware	4	2	50.00	1	50.00	2	50.00
Dist. of Columbia	1	1	100.00	0	0.00	0	0.00
Florida	34	23	67.65	18	78.26	11	32.35
Georgia	24	11	45.83	9	81.82	13	54.17
Hawaii	1	1	100.00	0	0.00	0	0.00
Idaho	4	1	25.00	1	100.00	3	75.00
Illinois	16	4	25.00	3	75.00	12	75.00
Indiana	15	8	53.33	7	87.50	7	46.67
Iowa	6	5	83.33	3	60.00	1	16.67
Kansas	6	4	66.67	2	50.00	2	33.33
Kentucky	7	3	42.86	2	66.67	4	57.14
Louisiana	21	3	14.29	1	33.33	18	85.71
Maine	0	0	0.00	0	0.00	0	0.00
Maryland	16	13	81.25	9	69.23	3	18.75
Massachusetts	9	9	100.00	6	66.67	0	0.00
Michigan	23	11	47.83	8	72.73	12	52.17
Minnesota	13	11	84.62	8	72.73	2	15.38
Mississippi	4	0	0.00	0	0.00	4	100.00
Missouri	16	11	68.75	9	81.82	5	31.25
Montana	1	0	0.00	0	0.00	1	100.00
Nebraska	3	2	66.67	2	100.00	1	33.33

continued

TABLE 1 (continued)

State	School Districts Serving 10,000+ Students N	School Districts with Multicultural Education Programs N	%	School Districts Responding to Survey N	%	School Districts with No Multicultural Education Programs N	%
Nevada	2	2	100.00	2	100.00	0	0.00
New Hampshire	2	1	50.00	1	100.00	1	50.00
New Jersey	11	7	63.64	5	71.43	4	36.36
New Mexico	7	6	85.71	5	83.33	1	16.67
New York	12	7	58.33	4	57.14	5	41.67
North Carolina	30	12	40.00	10	83.33	18	63.33
North Dakota	2	2	100.00	2	100.00	0	0.00
Ohio	18	10	55.56	10	100.00	8	44.44
Oklahoma	10	5	50.00	5	100.00	5	50.00
Oregon	8	6	75.00	3	50.00	2	25.00
Pennsylvania	12	6	50.00	4	66.67	6	50.00
Rhode Island	2	0	0.00	0	0.00	2	100.00
South Carolina	18	6	33.33	5	83.33	12	72.22
South Dakota	2	1	50.00	1	100.00	1	50.00
Tennessee	14	5	35.71	5	100.00	9	64.29
Texas	75	19	25.33	15	78.95	56	74.67
Utah	12	6	50.00	5	83.33	6	50.00
Vermont	0	0	0.00	0	0.00	0	0.00
Virginia	21	9	42.86	7	77.78	12	57.14
Washington	26	16	61.54	13	81.25	10	38.46
West Virginia	8	6	75.00	3	50.00	2	25.00
Wisconsin	8	5	62.50	5	100.00	3	37.50
Wyoming	2	0	0.00	0	0.00	2	100.00
Totals	713	329	46.14	255	77.08	384	53.86

TABLE 2
Multicultural Education Programs by State, 1995 & 1974

State	1995			1974			Change in Number of School Districts with Multicultural Education Programs, 1974-1995
	School Districts Serving 10,000+ Students N	School Districts with Multicultural Education Programs N	%	School Districts Serving 10,000+ Students N	School Districts with Multicultural Education Programs N	%	N
Alabama	12	3	25.0	13	5	38.5	-2
Alaska	3	2	66.7	2	2	100.0	0
Arizona	18	9	50.0	8	6	75.0	+3
Arkansas	3	3	100.0	4	3	75.0	0
California	128	39	30.5	113	61	54.0	-22
Colorado	18	9	50.0	11	8	72.7	+1
Connecticut	5	4	80.0	15	7	46.7	-3
Delaware	4	2	50.0	2	2	100.0	0
Dist. of Columbia	1	1	100.0	1	1	100.0	0
Florida	34	23	67.7	23	13	56.5	+10
Georgia	24	11	45.8	15	7	46.7	+4
Hawaii	1	1	100.0	1	1	100.0	0
Idaho	4	1	25.0	2	2	100.0	-1
Illinois	16	4	25.0	22	14	63.6	-10
Indiana	15	8	53.3	22	16	72.7	-8
Iowa	6	5	83.3	7	5	71.4	0
Kansas	6	4	66.7	5	3	60.0	+1
Kentucky	7	3	42.9	4	2	50.0	-1
Louisiana	21	3	14.3	20	10	50.0	-7
Maine	0	0	0.0	1	1	100.0	-1
Maryland	16	13	81.3	14	8	57.1	+5
Massachusetts	9	9	100.0	18	4	22.2	+5
Michigan	23	11	47.8	33	23	69.7	-12
Minnesota	13	11	84.6	16	12	75.0	-1
Mississippi	4	0	0.0	6	1	16.7	-1
Missouri	16	11	68.8	17	9	52.9	+2
Montana	1	0	0.0	2	1	50.0	-1

continued

TABLE 2 (continued)

State	1995 School Districts Serving 10,000+ Students N	School Districts with Multicultural Education Programs N	%	1974 School Districts Serving 10,000+ Students N	School Districts with Multicultural Education Programs N	%	Change in Number of School Districts with Multicultural Education Programs, 1974-1995 N
Nebraska	3	2	66.7	3	3	100.0	-1
Nevada	2	2	100.0	2	2	100.0	0
New Hampshire	2	1	50.0	1	0	0.0	+1
New Jersey	11	7	63.6	18	2	11.1	+5
New Mexico	7	6	85.7	5	4	80.0	+2
New York	12	7	58.3	38	12	31.6	-5
North Carolina	30	12	40.0	33	18	54.6	-6
North Dakota	2	2	100.0	3	2	66.7	0
Ohio	18	10	55.6	29	25	86.1	-15
Oklahoma	10	5	50.0	6	3	50.0	+2
Oregon	8	6	75.0	4	2	50.0	+4
Pennsylvania	12	6	50.0	31	17	54.8	-11
Rhode Island	2	0	0.0	4	3	75.0	-3
South Carolina	18	6	33.3	19	6	31.6	0
South Dakota	2	1	50.0	2	2	100.0	-1
Tennessee	14	5	35.7	11	7	63.6	-2
Texas	75	19	25.3	45	21	46.7	-2
Utah	12	6	50.0	7	5	71.4	+1
Vermont	0	0	0.0	0	0	0.0	0
Virginia	21	9	42.9	19	11	57.6	-2
Washington	26	16	61.5	15	6	40.0	+10
West Virginia	8	6	75.0	12	8	66.7	-2
Wisconsin	8	5	62.5	14	10	71.4	-5
Wyoming	2	0	0.0	2	1	50.0	-1
Totals	713	329	46.1	720	397	55.1	-68

TABLE 3
Multicultural Education Programs by Region, 1995 & 1974

	1995			1974			Change in Number of School Districts with Multicultural Education Programs, 1974-1995
State	School Districts Serving 10,000+ Students N	School Districts with Multicultural Education Programs N	%	School Districts Serving 10,000+ Students N	School Districts with Multicultural Education Programs N	%	N
New England (Connecticut, Maine, Massachusetts, New Hampshire, Rhode Island, Vermont)	18	14	77.8	39	15	34.3	-1
Middle Atlantic (Delaware, District of Columbia, Maryland, New Jersey, New York, Pennsylvania, West Virginia)	64	42	65.6	116	50	43.1	-8
Central (Kansas, Nebraska, North Dakota, Oklahoma, South Dakota)	23	14	60.9	19	13	68.4	+1
Mid-West (Illinois, Indiana, Iowa, Michigan, Minnesota, Missouri, Ohio, Wisconsin)	115	65	56.5	160	114	71.3	-49
Rocky Mountain (Arizona, Colorado, Idaho, Montana, Nevada, New Mexico, Utah, Wyoming)	64	33	51.6	39	29	74.4	+4
Pacific (Alaska, California, Hawaii, Oregon, Washington)	166	64	38.7	135	72	53.3	-8
South (Alabama, Arkansas, Florida, Georgia, Kentucky, Louisiana, Mississippi, North Carolina, South Carolina, Tennessee, Virginia)	263	97	36.9	212	104	49.1	-7
Totals	**713**	**329**	**46.1**	**720**	**397**	**55.1**	**-68**

CHAPTER FOUR

The Status of Multicultural
Education in the United States

I N 1974 FORTY-FOUR PERCENT OF THE LARGEST SCHOOL DISTRICTS IN THE
United States (those serving student populations of 10,000 or more)
were found in the twenty states of the New England, Middle Atlantic,
and Mid-Western regions and 56% in the remaining thirty states of the
Central, Rocky Mountain, Pacific, and Southern regions. By 1995, the
former industrial heartland of the country extending from the northeast
to the mid-west had come to be known as the "rustbelt." This "rustbelt"
now houses only 28% of the country's largest school districts, whereas
the "sunbelt" contains 72%. Those states gaining the most large districts
are Texas (thirty), California (fifteen), Florida (eleven), Washington
(eleven), and Arizona (eighteen). The big losers are New York (twenty-
six), Pennsylvania (nineteen), Ohio (eleven), Connecticut (ten), and
Michigan (ten).

With these demographic shifts have come changes in the delivery of
multicultural education to students of the largest school districts in the
United States. The 720 school districts Washburn surveyed in 1974 are
not precisely the same districts represented in the 1995 sample of the
713 districts now serving 10,000 or more students. This study provides
a picture of the present status of multicultural education in the United

States' largest districts and a comparison with the largest districts of 1974. Any changes that have occurred over this twenty-one year period are, in part, influenced by the demographic shifts which have occurred during those years and do not simply represent changes in the multicultural education programs of specific districts.

Regional Variations

Of the 713 school districts surveyed in 1995, all of which responded, 329 or 46.1% reported multicultural education programs. In 1974, 397 of the 720 districts (55.1%) had multicultural education programs. This is a significant change (at the .01 level) in a downward direction for multicultural education (*see* **Significance of the Difference Between Percentages** in the GLOSSARY). By region, the Mid-West, which lost forty-five large school districts, saw a forty-nine school district decline in multicultural education programs (TABLE 3). The Middle Atlantic region dropped fifty-two large school districts and eight multicultural education programs. New England's large school districts were reduced by twenty-one and their multicultural education programs by one. On the other hand, the South gained fifty-one large school districts, but lost seven multicultural education programs. The Pacific region added thirty-one school districts with 10,000 or more students and dropped eight multicultural education programs. Large school districts increased by twenty-five in the Rocky Mountain states and added four multicultural education programs. The Central region went up by four districts and one multicultural education program.

The states showing the most substantial gains in multicultural education among their large school districts (TABLE 2) were Florida (ten), Washington (ten), Massachusetts (five), Maryland (five), and New Jersey (five). California exhibited a decline of twenty-two multicultural education programs, followed by Ohio (fifteen), Illinois (ten), Indiana (eight), and Louisiana (seven).

Program Characteristics

Two programs have been in operation for thirty years (TABLE 4). The average length of operation for the 1995 programs was 7.6 years with a median of five years. In 1974 the mean and median were four years. The mode for both 1995 and 1974 was three years.

Those school districts which have programs tend to involve most or all of the grade levels (TABLE 5) and be focused on all students. Two hundred twenty-four school districts (87.8%) target all of their students with their multicultural education programs, whereas four (1.6%) focus on low achieving students and twenty-three (9%) on minority students alone. In 1974, mostly the higher grade levels and fewer students were involved. The average district in 1974 had 3,001 to 4,000 students participating with a median of 901-1,000, whereas the 1995 programs served on the average from 15,000 to 19,999 students with a median of 10,000 to 14,999 (TABLE 6).

The 1995 large school districts with multicultural education programs have, on the average, slightly higher percentages of African American, Asian/Pacific Islander American, Hispanic (Chicano/Latino) American, Native American, and other minority ethnic groups in their student populations than those in 1974, although the mean populations for each is still under 10% of the total student populations. The average European American (White Non-Hispanic) student population has fallen slightly (from 61-70% to 51-60%). There have been no significant changes in the ethnic composition of administrative staffs (71-80% European American), instructional staffs (81-90% European American), and support staffs (51-60% European American).

School Practices

In contrasting the responses received from the 255 school districts (77.08% of the 329 which reported having multicultural education programs in 1995) with the 397 school districts responding in 1974, we find some significant changes in the school practices employed (TABLE 13). Significantly higher (at the .01 level) proportions of the 1995 school districts have inservice teacher training in multicultural education, community involvement in school policy decisions, strong school-community public relations efforts, inter-racial student councils, human relations training for students, professionally staffed community relations offices, bilingual curricula, instruction in standard English as a second dialect, multilingual curricula, and instruction in Asian languages as second languages. A significant drop has, however, occurred in ethnic studies curricula (72.5% in 1974 to 48.6% in 1995). In 1995, of those districts reporting multicultural education programs and responding to our questionnaire, 123 reported ethnic studies curricula, whereas 288 of the 1974 respondents had ethnic studies curricula.

The changes in the programs of the school districts with ethnic studies curricula tend to favor the 1995 programs, although they are much fewer in number (**TABLE 14**). The 1974 programs had significantly more student involvement in curriculum planning, however. The groups included in ethnic studies have not changed much over the years (**TABLE 15**). African Americans are still the most widely studied group, followed by Hispanic (Latino/Chicano) Americans, Native Americans, and Asian/Pacific Islander Americans, in that order. There tends to be less study of European American groups than in 1974 with a significant drop in the inclusion of Slavic Americans in ethnic studies curricula. Social studies, language arts, English, art, music, and foreign languages are the disciplines most highly involved in ethnic studies (**TABLE 16**). There is significantly less study of ethnic history than in 1974, although 81.3% of the 1994 programs still include it (**TABLE 17**). There is also significantly lower inclusion of the study of the material cultures and physical characteristics of ethnic groups, whereas the study of body language is significantly higher than in 1974. Over 70% of the school districts with ethnic studies curricula include literature, social customs, music, art, and beliefs as elements studied in their programs.

In 1974 there were both quantitative and qualitative differences in the overall multicultural education programs of those districts with and without ethnic studies curricula. The inclusion of ethnic studies tended to presage a broader and deeper commitment to multicultural education in general. That line of demarcation is not so evident in 1995, although there are a number of areas of significant difference between those districts which include ethnic studies in their programs and those which do not (**TABLE 18**).

As was true in 1974, there is a high degree of community involvement in contemporary public school multicultural education programs. Almost 81% of the respondents to the earlier study reported community involvement in their programs. In 1995, fully 92.9% of the programs involved the community in some manner. Of the 255 programs responding, 79.6% utilized human resources in the community; 77.6% had interaction with community organizations; 77.3% used community resources; 53.7% had community involvement in curriculum planning; 37.3% studied the community; and 19.2% had a community based instructional program (**TABLE 7**). Additionally, 52.5% of the districts have produced materials for use in their programs and 18% offer some of these materials for sale.[1]

Program Goals and Aims

In an effort to categorize present day multicultural education programs according to Sleeter and Grant's typology[2], we asked respondents to characterize the primary social goal, school goal, curricular aim, and instructional aim of their programs as well as to identify the aspects of the classroom they incorporated into their multicultural education endeavor.

Of the 255 districts reporting, 39.6% indicated that the social goal for their programs was to promote social equality and cultural pluralism, which Sleeter and Grant depict as a characteristic of *multicultural education*. This was closely followed by the *human relations* social goal of promoting tolerance and acceptance within present society advocated by 31.8% of the districts. The third most popular social goal, selected by 13.7% of the districts, was to promote equality and recognition of a particular group or groups, which, according to Sleeter and Grant, is a trait of *single-group studies*. To help students fit into present society, a social goal typical of the *teaching the exceptional and culturally different* program type, was selected by 8.6% of the population. Only 3.9% of the districts had as their goal to promote active social change which will enhance the power position of oppressed peoples, a goal favored by proponents of the *education that is multicultural and social reconstructionist* position (**TABLE 8**).

Human relations and *multicultural education* school goals also predominate. The *human relations* school goal to promote positive feelings among students, reduce stereotyping, and promote students' self-concepts was chosen by 36.5% of the districts. To promote equal opportunity in the school, cultural pluralism, respect for those who differ, and support of power equality among groups, a *multicultural education* school goal, is the preference of 35.7% of the sample population. Nearly 14% of the school districts pick the preparation of citizens to work actively toward social equality, promote cultural pluralism and alternative lifestyles, and promote equal opportunity in the school, the school goal embraced by supporters of the *education that is multicultural and social reconstructionist* position. A remainder of 11.4% of the districts wish to teach students to become culturally literate by making the core disciplines relevant to their lives, a *teaching the exceptional and culturally different* position. No school district advocated the *single-group studies* school goal of developing in students the motivation and knowledge to work toward social change that would benefit their particular group (TABLE 9).

When it came to the programs' curricular and instructional aims, *multicultural education* held the ascendant position it was granted by school districts in their selection of social and school goals, but the *human relations* approach fell to fourth place. Forty percent of the population had the teaching of the contributions and perspectives of several different groups, critical thinking, analyses of alternative viewpoints, making the curriculum relevant to students' experiential backgrounds, and promotion of the use of more than one language or dialect as their curricular aim. Corresponding to this *multicultural education* position was the instructional aim to build on the students' learning styles, adapt to their skill levels, involve them actively in thinking and analyzing, and use cooperative learning, adopted by 43.1% of the respondents. Second among school districts' curricular and instructional aims for their multicultural education programs was the *education that is multicultural and social reconstructionist* curricular aim to teach current social issues involving racism, classism, sexism, and handicapism; teach experiences and perspectives of several different American groups; use students' life experiences as a starting point for analyzing oppression; teach critical thinking, analysis of alternative viewpoints, social action, and empowerment; and the instructional aim to involve students actively in democratic decision making; build on students' learning styles; adapt to students' skill levels; use cooperative learning; and develop a spirit of social activism. Fourteen percent of the programs elected as their curricular aim to make the curriculum relevant to students' experiential backgrounds and fill in gaps in basic skills and knowledge; and the instructional aim to build on students' learning styles, adapt to their skill levels, and teach as effectively and efficiently as possible to enable students to catch up; which are aims characteristic of the *teaching the exceptional and culturally different* position. The *human relations* aims of teaching lessons about stereotyping, name-calling, individual differences and similarities, and contributions of groups of which students are members; and using cooperative learning, and real or vicarious experiences with others; were chosen by 11% and 6.7%, respectively. The *single-group studies* approaches of teaching units or courses about the culture of a particular group, how the group has been victimized, and current social issues facing the group from the perspective of that group (a curricular aim of 4.3% of the programs); and building on the learning style of the students' group (an instructional aim of 2.7% of the districts) were the least popular among the school districts responding (TABLES 10 AND 11).

A wide array of aspects of the classroom are incorporated into the multicultural education programs of the 255 districts answering our questionnaire, representing a full range of approaches advocated by each of the categorical designations of Sleeter and Grant's typology (TABLE 12).

Multicultural Versus Non-Multicultural Goals and Aims

In an effort to discern whether the selection of social and school goals and curricular and instructional aims had significant effects on programmatic elements of school districts' multicultural education endeavors, we combined Sleeter and Grant's *teaching the exceptional and culturally different, human relations,* and *single-group studies* into a designation we termed *non-multicultural*. Our rationale for this designation rests upon the notion that the first two types are designed to help people adjust to present conditions and that the status quo is anglo-conformist. So the *teaching the exceptional and culturally different* approaches, if successful, will allow people to fit into and accept an anglo-conformist social structure and the *human relations* approach will help them feel good about it. Further, *single-group studies* focusing on *one* group can by no means be designated *multi*cultural. On the other hand, we specified as *multicultural* Sleeter and Grant's *multicultural education* and *education that is multicultural and social reconstructionist* types because they are designed to prepare people for effective participation in a culturally pluralistic social environment or the creation of a more just, humane, equitable, and democratic pluralism.

Utilizing the Statistical Package for the Social Studies (SPSS), we did a cross-tabulation for each of the variables measured by our survey instrument of *multicultural* versus *non-multicultural* social goals, school goals, curricular aims, and instructional aims. Significant differences (at the .05 level or above) were noted.

As might be expected, programs with *multicultural social goals* are significantly more likely to have multicultural school goals, and curricular and instructional aims. They are much more likely to decorate classrooms to reflect multiculturalism and social reconstructionism; to use library materials reflecting diversity; to have inservice teacher training in multicultural education (although a large percentage of all school districts engage in this practice); to have an inter-racial student council; a student human relations council; a bicultural and multilingual curriculum; instruction in standard English as a second dialect; and school district produced materials available for purchase (TABLE 19).

Those districts with *multicultural school goals* are more likely to engage in study of the community; interact with community organizations; have multicultural social goals and curricular and instructional aims; decorate classrooms to reflect multiculturalism and social reconstructionism; involve minority parents in school policy decisions; have an inter-racial student council; and a student human relations council (TABLE 20).

The agenda of school districts with *multicultural curricular aims* exhibit significant differences with those who offer *non-multicultural curricular aims*. Only seventy-five districts are included in the latter populations, however. The former group is more likely to study the community; have multicultural social and school goals and instructional aims; target all students for their multicultural education programs; decorate classrooms to reflect multiculturalism and social reconstructionism; employ faculty from groups studied; involve minority parents in school policy decisions; have diversity based staffing patterns; use library materials reflecting diversity; have the school involved in local community action projects; have the community involved in school policy decisions; have student involvement in school policy decisions; have a bilingual curriculum; have a student human relations council; have a bicultural curriculum; and have school district produced materials for the program. Conversely, they are *less likely* to target just low achieving and minority students for their programs than programs we have designated as having *non-multicultural curricular aims* (TABLE 21).

School districts with *multicultural instructional aims* (which includes 198 of the 255 programs) are more likely to have multicultural goals and aims; decorate classrooms to reflect multiculturalism; offer school-wide activities aimed at peace and unity; use library materials reflecting diversity; have school buildings accessible to disabled people; have the school involved in local community action projects; have inservice teacher training in multicultural education; and have a student human relations council (TABLE 22).

Summary

Although demographic changes may be partly responsible, there has been a significant drop in multicultural education programs among the country's largest school districts since 1974. All regions of the United States, except the Central (which has gained one) and Rocky Mountain (which has gained four) had fewer programs in 1995 than twenty-one years earlier. The average length of programs operative in 1995 was 7.6 years. Although there are fewer programs, significantly more grade levels and students on a per program basis are presently involved in multicultural education than in 1974. The minority student populations are slightly higher and the European American student populations slightly lower now than before. The contemporary programs are more thorough and involved in a broader range of multicultural school practices than the earlier programs, except for a significant drop in ethnic studies curricula. The modern ethnic studies curricula are equally as focused on minority groups and somewhat less focused on European American ethnic groups than the earlier curricula. Community involvement is still a feature of multicultural education. The current programs tend to have *multicultural* and *human relations* social and school goals, whereas the curricular and instructional aims are predominantly *multicultural and social reconstructionist* in orientation. The districts with multicultural education programs, by and large, decorate classrooms to focus on representatives of groups and student accomplishments, and to reflect multicultural and social reconstructionist themes. Those districts whose goals and aims are *multicultural* or *social reconstructionist* exhibit some areas of significant differences in their programs when compared with districts whose goals and aims focus more on *human relations, educating the exceptional and culturally different*, or *single-group studies*.

TABLE 4

Length of Operation of Multicultural Education Programs, 1995
(N=255)

	Years	Number of Districts	Percentage
	Less than 1	32	12.5
	1	24	9.4
	2	13	5.1
	3	32	12.5
	4	24	9.4
1995	5	25	9.8
Mean=7.6 years	6	14	5.5
Median=5.0	7	4	1.6
Mode=3	8	7	2.7
	9	3	1.2
	10	15	5.9
1974	11	4	1.6
Mean=4.0 years	12	5	2.0
Median=4.0	13	2	.8
Mode=3	14	2	.8
	15	4	1.6
	16	2	.8
	17	1	.4
	18	4	1.6
	20	17	6.7
	21	2	.8
	22	6	2.4
	23	3	1.2
	25	2	.8
	30	2	.8
	no response	6	2.4

TABLE 5

Grade Levels Involved in Multicultural Education Programs, 1995
(N=255)

Grade	Number of Districts	Percentage
K	218	85.5
1	222	87.1
2	223	87.5
3	224	87.8
4	225	88.2
5	226	88.6
6	226	88.6
7	222	87.1
8	219	85.9
9	227	89.0
10	224	87.8
11	226	88.6
12	227	89.0

TABLE 6
Number of Students Participating in
Multicultural Education Programs, 1995
(N=255)

Number of Students	Number of Districts	Percentage
c0-4,999	78	30.6
5,000-9,999	9	3.5
b10,000-14,999	52	20.4
a15,000-19,999	26	10.2
20,000-24,999	18	7.1
25,000-29,999	20	7.8
30,000-34,999	8	3.1
35,000-39,999	3	1.2
40,000-44,999	6	2.4
50,000-54,999	5	2.0
55,000-59,999	5	2.0
60,000-64,999	3	1.2
65,000-69,999	1	.4
70,000-74,999	2	.8
80,000-84,999	4	1.6
over 100,000	8	3.1
no response	7	2.7

a=mean   **b**=median   **c**=mode

TABLE 7
Extent and Type of Community Involvement
in Multicultural Education Programs, 1995
(N=255)

Type of Community Involvement	Number of Districts	Percentage
Use of Human Resources in Community	203	79.6
Interaction with Community Organizations	198	77.6
Use of Community Resources	197	77.3
Community Involvement in Curriculum Planning	137	53.7
Study of the Community	95	37.3
Community-based Instructional Program	49	19.2

TABLE 8

Social Goals for Multicultural Education Programs, 1995
(N=255)

Social Goal	Number of Districts	Percentage
Promote Social Equality and Cultural Pluralism (*Multicultural Education*)	101	39.6
Promote Tolerance and Acceptance within Present Society (*Human Relations*)	81	31.8
Promote Equality and Recognition of a Particular Group or Groups (*Single-Group Studies*)	35	13.7
Help Students Fit into Present Society (*Teaching the Exceptional and Culturally Different*)	22	8.6
Promote Active Social Change which will Enhance the Power Position of Oppressed Peoples (*Education that is Multicultural and Social Reconstructionist*)	10	3.9
no response	6	2.4

TABLE 9

School Goals for Multicultural Education Programs, 1995
(N=255)

School Goal	Number of Districts	Percentage
Human Relations	93	36.5
Multicultural Education	91	35.7
Education that is Multicultural and Social Reconstructionist	35	13.7
Teaching the Exceptional and Culturally Different	29	11.4
Single-Group Studies	0	0.0
no response	7	2.8

TABLE 10
Curricular Aims of Multicultural Education Programs, 1995
(N=255)

Curricular Aim	Number of Districts	Percentage
Multicultural Education	102	40.0
Education that is Multicultural and Social Reconstructionist	73	28.6
Teaching the Exceptional and Culturally Different	36	14.1
Human Relations	28	11.0
Single-Group Studies	11	4.3
no response	5	2.0

TABLE 11
Instructional Aims of Multicultural Education Programs, 1995
(N=255)

Instructional Aim	Number of Districts	Percentage
Multicultural Education	110	43.1
Education that is Multicultural and Social Reconstructionist	88	34.5
Teaching the Exceptional and Culturally Different	23	9.0
Human Relations	17	6.7
Single-Group Studies	7	2.7
no response	10	3.9

TABLE 12

Aspects of the Classroom Incorporated
into Multicultural Education Programs, 1995
(N=255)

Aspect of Classroom	Number of Districts	Percentage
Use Decorations Reflecting Cultural Contributions of a Particular Group (*Single-Group Studies*)	180	70.6
Use Decorations Showing Group Members Integrated into Mainstream of Society (*Teaching the Exceptional and Culturally Different*)	161	63.1
Decorate Classroom to Reflect Uniqueness and Accomplishments of Students (*Human Relations*)	154	60.4
Decorate Classroom to Reflect Cultural Pluralism, Nontraditional Sex Roles, Disabled People, and Student Interests (*Multicultural Education*)	153	60.0
Decorate Classroom to Reflect Social Action Themes, Cultural Diversity, and Aspects of Society that Need to be Changed in Order to Achieve Equal Justice for All (*Education that is Multicultural and Social Reconstructionist*)	135	52.9

TABLE 13

School Practices Incorporated into
Multicultural Education Programs, 1995 & 1974

School Practice	1995 Percentage (N=255)	1974 Percentage (N=397)
Community Involvement in Program	92.9	—
Use of Library Materials which Portray Groups in Diverse Roles	91.4	—
•Inservice Teacher Training in Multicultural Education	85.5	49.4
Include All Student Groups in Extra-Curricular Activities	83.9	—

continued

TABLE 13 (continued)

School Buildings Accessible to Disabled People	83.5	—
English as a Second Language	82.7	—
Activities, Policies, and Practices which Do Not "Put Down" or Leave Out Some Groups of Students	82.0	—
Decorations, Special Events, School Menus Reflect and Include Diverse Groups	78.0	—
•Community Involvement in School Policy Decisions	76.1	61.5
Discipline Procedures Do Not Penalize Any Particular Group	76.1	—
School-Wide Activities Aimed at Peace and Unity	71.4	—
Involve Lower-Class and Minority Parents in Decisions Concerning School Policies and Practices	69.8	—
School Involved in Local Community Action Projects	69.0	—
•A Strong School-Community Public Relations Effort	68.2	52.9
Human Relations Training for Teachers	66.3	66.8
Employ Faculty Who are Members of the Group or Groups Being Studied	65.1	—
Involve Lower-Class and Minority Parents in Supporting Work of the School	64.7	—
Student Involvement in Democratic Decision-Making About Substantive School-Wide Concerns	55.7	—

continued

TABLE 13 (continued)

•An Inter-Racial Student Council	52.5	37.0
Staffing Pattern Includes Diverse Racial, Gender, and Disability Groups	52.5	—
•Human Relations Training for Students	51.0	32.0
Remedial Classes	50.6	—
Instruction in Spanish as a Second Language	49.0	43.6
•An Ethnic Studies Curriculum	48.6	72.5
Transitional Bilingual Education	47.8	—
Student Involvement in School Policy Decisions	45.5	40.6
Special Education as Temporary and Intensive Aids to Fill Gaps in Knowledge	43.5	—
•A Professionally Staffed Community Relations Office	40.4	29.2
•A Bilingual Curriculum	37.6	26.2
•Student Involvement in Curriculum Planning	27.5	44.8
•Instruction in Standard English as a Second Dialect	26.3	5.8
•A Multilingual Curriculum	24.7	7.8
A Bicultural Curriculum	23.5	17.4
A Professionally Staffed Human Relations Team	23.5	22.9
•Instruction in Asian Language(s) as Second Language(s)	18.0	4.5
A Student Human Relations Council	15.3	21.2
Instruction in Native American Language(s) as Second language(s)	5.9	2.3

• *These Differences are Significant at the .01 Level*

TABLE 14
School Practices Reported by School
Districts with Ethnic Studies Curricula, 1995 & 1974

School Practice	1995 Percentage (N=123)	1974 Percentage (N=288)
•Inservice Teacher Training in Multicultural Education	91.9	56.6
•Instruction in English as a Second Language	83.7	37.8
Community Involvement in School Policy Decisions	78.4	69.8
Human Relations Training for Teachers	74.0	74.0
•A Strong School-Community Public Relations Effort	72.4	58.0
•An Inter-Racial Student Council	60.2	43.4
Instruction in Spanish as a Second Language	54.5	49.7
•Human Relations Training for Students	53.7	36.5
Student Involvement in School Policy Decisions	46.3	47.2
A Professionally Staffed Community Relations Office	46.3	34.4
•A Bilingual Curriculum	44.7	30.6
•Student Involvement in Curriculum Planning	34.1	53.1
A Professionally Staffed Human Relations Team	34.1	29.5
•Instruction in Standard English as a Second Dialect	33.3	6.9
•A Multilingual Curriculum	31.7	10.4
A Bicultural Curriculum	30.1	22.2
A Community Centered Instructional Program	25.2	30.6
A Student Human Relations Council	21.1	24.7
•Instruction in Asian Language(s) as Second Language(s)	21.1	5.2
Instruction in Native American Language(s) as Second Language(s)	9.8	2.8

• *These Differences are Significant at the .01 Level*

TABLE 15
Groups Included in Ethnic Studies Curricula, 1995 & 1974

Group	1995 (N=123) Districts	%	1974 (N=288) Districts	%
African Americans	104	84.6	265	92.0
Hispanic (Latino/Chicano) Americans	86	69.9	203	70.5
Native Americans	76	61.8	193	67.0
Asian/Pacific Islander Americans	72	58.5	142	49.3
Arab Americans	27	22.0	—	—
German Americans	27	22.0	86	29.9
French Americans	25	20.3	75	26.0
Italian Americans	24	19.5	90	31.3
Irish Americans	23	18.7	85	29.5
Greek Americans	19	15.4	—	—
Iranian Americans	12	9.8	—	—
•Slavic Americans	12	9.8	72	25.0
Scandinavian Americans	10	8.1	—	—
Portuguese Americans	9	7.3	—	—

• *This Difference is Significant at the .01 Level*

TABLE 16
Disciplines Participating in Ethnic Studies Curricula, 1995 (N=123)

Discipline	Number of Districts	Percentage
Social Studies	106	86.2
Language Arts	86	69.9
English	70	56.9
Art	69	56.6
Music	66	53.7
Foreign Languages	65	52.8
Reading	59	48.0
Humanities	48	39.0
Science	39	31.7
Mathematics	37	30.1
Physical Education	32	26.0
Theater	32	26.0
Home Economics	30	24.4
Health	26	21.1
Business	19	15.4
Industrial Arts	19	15.4

TABLE 17

Elements Included in Ethnic Studies Curricula, 1995 & 1974

Element	1995 (N=123)		1974 (N=288)	
	Districts	%	Districts	%
•History	100	81.3	273	94.8
Literature	94	76.4	—	—
Social Customs	94	76.4	238	82.6
Music	92	74.8	—	—
Art	91	74.0	—	—
Beliefs	87	71.3	170	59.0
Culture and Personality	86	69.9	206	71.5
Foods	85	69.1	—	—
•Body Language	83	68.0	54	18.8
Language	73	59.3	145	50.3
Attitudes	71	58.2	185	64.2
Values	69	56.1	198	68.8
Social Structure	66	53.7	176	61.1
Social Organization	64	52.0	180	62.5
Religion	63	51.2	161	55.9
•Material Culture	45	36.6	182	63.2
Drama	44	35.8	—	—
Kinship Structure	43	35.0	87	30.2
•Physical Characteristics	37	30.1	129	44.8
Dialect	36	29.5	76	26.4

• *These Differences are Significant at the .01 Level*

TABLE 18

Areas of Significant Differences: School Districts With or Without Ethnic Studies Curricula, 1995

Area	Districts With Ethnic Studies (N=123) %	Districts Without Ethnic Studies (N=132) %	Level of Significant Difference
African American Student Population	11-20	0-10	.01
European American Student Population	41-50	61-70	.05
European American Administrative Population	61-70	81-90	.03
European American Instructional Population	61-70	81-90	.03
Community-Based Instructional Program	25.2	13.8	.05
Decorate Classrooms to Reflect Contributions of a Particular Group	77.2	64.6	.04
Decorate Classrooms to Reflect Multiculturalism and Social Reconstructionism	65.9	41.5	.01
Transitional Bilingual Education	56.1	39.2	.01
Diversity-Based Staffing Patterns	60.2	45.4	.03
Human Relations Training for Teachers	74.0	59.2	.02
Inservice Teacher Training in Multicultural Education	91.9	80.8	.02
Student Involvement in Curriculum Planning	34.1	20.8	.03
An Inter-Racial Student Council	60.2	44.6	.02
A Bilingual Curriculum	44.7	30.8	.03
A Professionally Staffed Human Relations Team	34.1	13.8	.01
A Student Human Relations Council	21.0	10.0	.02
A Bicultural Curriculum	30.1	17.1	.02
A Multilingual Curriculum	31.7	18.6	.02
Instruction in Standard English as a Second Dialect	33.3	19.2	.02
Instruction in Native American Languages as Second Languages	9.8	2.3	.03
School Produced Materials for Program	64.8	41.5	.01
School Produced Materials Available for Purchase	23.8	12.3	.02

TABLE 19

Areas of Significant Differences: School Districts With Multicultural or Non-Multicultural Social Goals, 1995

Area	Districts With Multicultural Social Goals• (N=111) %	Districts With Non-Multicultural Social Goals•• (N=138) %	Level of Significant Difference
Non-Multicultural School Goals	26.1	67.4	.05
Multicultural School Goals	73.9	31.2	.05
Non-Multicultural Curricular Aims	18.0	39.9	.05
Multicultural Curricular Aims	81.1	60.1	.05
Non-Multicultural Instructional Aims	9.9	26.1	.05
Multicultural Instructional Aims	89.2	71.0	.05
Decorate Classrooms to Reflect Multiculturalism	72.1	50.0	.01
Decorate Classrooms to Reflect Multiculturalism and Social Reconstructionism	64.0	44.2	.01
Use of Library Materials Reflecting Diversity	96.4	87.7	.03
Inservice Teacher Training in Multicultural Education	91.0	82.6	.03
An Inter-Racial Student Council	63.1	43.5	.01
A Student Human Relations Council	21.6	8.7	.01
A Bicultural Curriculum	30.9	18.8	.04
A Multilingual Curriculum	32.7	19.6	.03
Instruction in Standard English as a Second Dialect	34.2	21.0	.03
School District Produced Materials Available for Purchase	25.5	12.3	.04

• Multicultural Social Goals=Goals compatible with Sleeter and Grant's *Multicultural Education* and *Education that is Multicultural and Social Reconstructionist.*
•• Non-Multicultural Social Goals=Goals compatible with Sleeter and Grant's *Teaching the Exceptional and Culturally Different*, *Human Relations*, and *Single-Group Studies.*

TABLE 20

Areas of Significant Differences: School Districts With Multicultural or Non-Multicultural School Goals, 1995

Area	Districts With Multicultural School Goals• (N=126) %	Districts With Non-Multicultural School Goals•• (N=122) %	Level of Significant Difference
Study of the Community	45.2	31.1	.04
Interaction with Community Organizations	85.7	72.1	.04
Non-Multicultural Social Goals	31.2	76.2	.01
Multicultural Social Goals	65.1	27.8	.01
Non-Multicultural Curricular Aims	17.5	43.4	.01
Multicultural Curricular Aims	81.7	56.6	.01
Non-Multicultural Instructional Aims	17.5	43.4	.01
Multicultural Instructional Aims	81.7	56.6	.01
Decorate Classrooms to Reflect Multiculturalism	69.0	50.0	.01
Decorate Classrooms to Reflect Multiculturalism and Social Reconstructionism	64.3	41.8	.01
Involve Minority Parents in School Policy Decisions	77.6	62.3	.03
An Inter-Racial Student Council	58.6	41.8	.01
A Student Human Relations Council	19.0	9.0	.01

• Multicultural School Goals=Goals compatible with Sleeter and Grant's *Multicultural Education* and *Education that is Multicultural and Social Reconstructionist.*
•• Non-Multicultural School Goals=Goals compatible with Sleeter and Grant's *Teaching the Exceptional and Culturally Different, Human Relations,* and *Single-Group Studies.*

TABLE 21

Areas of Significant Differences: School Districts With Multicultural or Non-Multicultural Curricular Aims, 1995

Area	Districts With Multicultural Curricular Aims• (N=175) %	Districts With Non-Multicultural Curricular Aims•• (N=75) %	Level of Significant Difference
Study of the Community	42.9	26.7	.03
Non-Multicultural Social Goals	47.4	73.3	.01
Multicultural Social Goals	51.4	26.7	.01
Non-Multicultural School Goals	39.4	70.7	.01
Multicultural School Goals	58.9	29.3	.01
Non-Multicultural Instructional Aims	9.1	41.3	.01
Multicultural Instructional Aims	89.1	56.0	.01
Target Population: Low Achieving and Minority Students	6.3	21.3	.01
Target Population: All Students	93.7	78.7	.01
Decorate Classrooms to Reflect Multiculturalism	65.1	48.0	.04
Decorate Classrooms to Reflect Multiculturalism and Social Reconstructionism	61.1	34.7	.01
Employ Faculty from Groups Studied	72.0	50.7	.01
Involve Minority Parents in School Policy Decisions	75.9	57.3	.01
Diversity-Based Staffing Patterns	58.9	40.0	.02
Use of Library Materials Reflecting Diversity	94.9	84.0	.04
School Involved in Local Community Action Projects	74.3	56.0	.02
Community Involvement in School Policy Decisions	80.6	66.7	.03
Student Involvement in School Policy Decisions	50.3	33.3	.05
A Bilingual Curriculum	42.9	25.3	.03
A Student Human Relations Council	18.9	5.3	.01
A Bicultural Curriculum	28.7	13.3	.02
School District Produced Materials for Program	58.0	42.7	.03

• Multicultural Curricular Aims=Aims compatible with Sleeter and Grant's *Multicultural Education* and *Education that is Multicultural and Social Reconstructionist.*
•• Non-Multicultural Curricular Aims=Aims compatible with Sleeter and Grant's *Teaching the Exceptional and Culturally Different, Human Relations,* and *Single-Group Studies.*

TABLE 22

Areas of Significant Differences: School Districts With Multicultural or Non-Multicultural Instructional Aims, 1995

Area	Districts With Multicultural Instructional Aims• (N=198) %	Districts With Non-Multicultural Instructional Aims•• (N=47) %	Level of Significant Difference
Non-Multicultural Social Goals	49.5	76.6	.01
Multicultural Social Goals	50.0	23.4	.01
Non-Multicultural School Goals	47.0	57.4	.01
Multicultural School Goals	53.0	40.4	.01
Non-Multicultural Curricular Aims	21.2	66.0	.01
Multicultural Curricular Aims	78.8	34.0	.01
Decorate Classrooms to Reflect Multiculturalism	65.2	40.4	.01
School-Wide Activities Aimed at Peace and Unity	76.3	51.1	.01
Use of Library Materials Reflecting Diversity	93.9	83.0	.01
School Buildings Accessible to Disabled People	85.9	76.6	.05
School Involved in Local Community Action Projects	72.7	51.1	.01
Inservice Teacher Training in Multicultural Education	88.4	76.6	.03
A Student Human Relations Council	15.2	10.6	.04

• Multicultural Instructional Aims=Aims compatible with Sleeter and Grant's *Multicultural Education* and *Education that is Multicultural and Social Reconstructionist.*
•• Non-Multicultural Instructional Aims=Aims compatible with Sleeter and Grant's *Teaching the Exceptional and Culturally Different*, *Human Relations*, and *Single-Group Studies.*

CHAPTER FIVE

Reconceptualizing Multicultural Education for the Twenty-First Century[1]

IN SPITE OF THE GROWTH IN THE POPULATION OF MINORITY ETHNIC GROUPS and a burgeoning academic and theoretical literature on the topic of multicultural education, the practice of multicultural education among the largest school districts of the United States has diminished since 1974. Where multicultural education programs do exist, they tend to have a broader range than in 1974, however.[2] They involve more students at more grade levels. Social and school goals and curricular and instructional aims at these school districts are multicultural in nature. They incorporate a wide range of school and classroom practices reflective of a commitment to multicultural education. Many have developed materials for their programs and they utilize library resources which portray groups in diverse roles. They involve the community in their multicultural education endeavors and are involved in local community action projects. They engage their instructional and administrative personnel in inservice training for multicultural education. They provide English as a second language training for students. These districts decorate their schools, offer special events, and prepare school menus which reflect and include diverse groups. They proffer school-wide activities aimed at peace and unity, and involve lower-class and minority parents in decisions concerning school policies and practices. They keep diversity in mind when employing professional personnel.

Less than half of the 713 school districts which serve student populations of 10,000 or more have made a commitment to multicultural education, however. Obviously, the level of commitment of those districts involved in multicultural education varies as well. For instance, of the 329 districts with multicultural education programs, only 123 report having ethnic studies curricula. James A. Banks states, "The three decades between 1960 and 1990 were probably the most productive research period in ethnic studies in the nation's history."[3] If this be true, then it is shocking that ethnic studies content is not inextricably tied to the academic life of every school-aged child in the United States. Even among those school districts which display a level of commitment to multicultural education, only a minority offer ethnic studies curricula to students. What is the purpose of ethnic studies research and the development of multicultural education theory, if it is not to have an impact on the lives of citizens to the end of producing a greater understanding and sense of community among the peoples of the United States? There are considerably fewer ethnic studies curricula abroad in the land today than in 1974. Those that do exist are even less inclusive than those offered over two decades ago. The programs, then and now, focus on a few minority ethnic groups, and therefore, are more correctly characterized as minority studies rather than multicultural education. An argument can be made that *business as usual* in public education is so anglo-conformist in curricular orientation that a focus on European American studies is unnecessary. Even if this argument is accepted, it neglects the contributions made by those of central-, eastern-, and southern-European ancestry to our American mosaic. Their sensibilities have been given short shrift in the academic programs of our public education systems. They are doing less well, in this academic sense, now than in 1974. And, many other ethnic groups receive no mention at all in the vast majority of the instruction offered by the public schools of the United States. Further, ethnic studies, where it does exist, has a rather narrow band of disciplines involved in the curricula. Ethnic studies is perceived as the province of the social studies and, to a lesser extent, language arts. Other disciplines involved in over 50% of the 123 programs include English, art, music, and foreign languages. In this era of whole language and cooperative learning, are we not imaginative enough to involve all disciplines in multiethnic education? No matter how school districts deliver subject matter, be it through interdisciplinary thematic units or through a traditional disciplinary approach, ethnic studies content must be an essential element in the education of everyone who is to become a responsible participant in our culturally pluralistic democracy and multicultural world. We are studying less ethnic history and more cultural kinesics in contemporary curricula than in 1974. The gains we make in understanding the connections in body language to cultural group membership, thereby enhancing our ability to communicate across cultures, should not be at the expense of knowledge of groups' histories, beliefs, attitudes, values, religions, and material cultures.

Critical Evaluation

It appears that the brakes were put on the advances that were being made in multicultural education at the public school level during the 1970s. Half of the contemporary multicultural education programs are less than five years old and there are fewer programs today than in 1974. The 1980s, a time of great development in multicultural education theory, was a period of diminution in multicultural education practice. The continuing active conversation that academics were having about multicultural education did not result in programmatic development in the public schools, although those districts which are now making a commitment to multicultural education seem to be informed by theoretical developments in the field resulting in many exemplary endeavors.

Those within school districts who may not have had an abiding devotion to multicultural education in the first place were given an excuse to abandon their efforts by the federal government of the 1980s which was openly anglo-conformist. Shortly after the inauguration of President Ronald Reagan in 1981, the Ethnic Heritage Studies Act (Title IX of the Elementary and Secondary Education Act) was eliminated[4] and with it the Ethnic Heritage Branch of the United States Department of Education. Donna M. Gollnick wrote, that, by the early 1990s "...most federal legislation did not promote education that is multicultural. The primary focus was on...teaching the culturally different and students with disabilities."[5]

Apparently, government initiatives, if they are coupled with accountability, do make a difference in effectuating educational policy. Gollnick, in her analysis of approaches to multicultural education in state policies reports that in 1978 Iowa had passed legislation requiring the adoption of plans for multicultural education by local school boards. Although she indicates that by the 1990s state funding supporting the implementation of multicultural education in Iowa was no longer available[6], our data show that five of the six large school districts in that state have multicultural education programs. Of the states that Gollnick reports to have followed Iowa's lead, Maryland (thirteen of sixteen), Minnesota (eleven of thirteen), Nebraska (two of three), and New Jersey (seven of eleven), show high levels of involvement in multicultural education among their largest school districts. Delaware, which issued a comprehensive plan, but did not include an accountability system[7], has two of its four large districts reporting multicultural education programs. West Virginia, which requires counties to provide staff development in multicultural education[8], has six of eight large districts with programs. Arkansas (three of three), Connecticut (four of five), Kansas (four of six), Kentucky (three of seven), Michigan (eleven of twenty-three), Ohio (ten of eighteen), and Washington (sixteen of twenty-six), are the other states that have policies related to multicultural education.[9]

Viewing the status of multicultural education in the United States from the frameworks provided by Sleeter and Grant's typology[10] and through an adaptation of the work of Milton M. Gordon[11], we can discern that *business as usual*, or anglo-conformity, is the dominant ideology influencing educational policy today. Multicultural education in one form or another is practiced by a minority of large school districts. Can we expect that the demographic trend toward a more culturally heterogeneous United States will necessarily lead to a culturally pluralistic orientation for our public schools?

In most countries on this globe a small number of people control the life fates of the majority. It does not necessarily follow that simply because the United States will become a minority majority country during the twenty-first century that these groups will be shaping social policy at that time. But these projected changes do appear to have attracted the attention of today's power elite. Many of the anglo-conformist, assimilationist, essentialist educational policies articulated in *A Nation At Risk* and *America* (or *Goals*) *2000* reports have been promulgated from the Reagan, Bush, and Clinton White Houses through the state houses to schools. This could be perceived as cynical attempts to maintain the status quo by further tranquilizing the minds of young citizens and, thereby, producing a mass society who respond behaviorally with even greater enthusiasm to the crass propagandization of a narrowly focused power elite.

On the other hand, they may really believe their own propaganda, having been imbued with a conceptual orientation which places them at the authoritative center of a natural order (set by the invisible hand of a white male god, no doubt) in which values (Anglo-Saxon or Anglo-Teutonic values at that) are absolute and eternal, where it is their role to see that natural law should prevail unimpeded, and transcendent truths are transmitted to the uninitiated.

This latter possibility is the more disquieting for true believers can be much more dangerous with their backs to the wall than cynics. And, those advocating the culturally pluralistic orientations for the schools have it within their grasp to put myopic ethnocentrism to a very stern test.

The liberally pluralistic progressivist and the corporately pluralistic reconstructionist positions are more complex, their advocates speaking with disparate voices, their power less concentrated than the anglo-conformists, however. Those favoring a culturally pluralistic interpretation of United States national culture appear to share a number of premises which place them at odds with the anglo-conformists. Rather than a fixed exogenous reality independent from human intelligence they grasp an **anthropic cosmological** interpretation which holds that human intelligence is essential not only to the nature of the universe but to its very existence. Pluralism rests on a "many worlds" theory of reality in which the conceptualization of human groups is central. No matter what the universe may be in and of itself, its meaning is relative to the conceptualization of humans. In like manner, human groups create and test rules for living. These rules are contextual. Different groups create different rules which are tested in different cultural contexts. Knowledge and truth are contextual phenomena as well. One group's truth can be another group's myth. The relativism of cultural pluralism is in sharp contrast to the absolutistic notions of anglo-conformity.

Ultimately, which interpretation will be realized in social and educational policy formulation and implementation is more a matter of political power and national will than clarity of vision, however. People who tend to get their policies put into place are presently favoring an anglo-conformist approach, but the grass roots are increasingly multicultural. The role of policy becomes assimilation of the multicultural masses, through education and other means, into the anglo-conformist mainstream. However, the social reality is structural pluralism along ethclass lines with some acculturation and assimilation at the various margins.

The liberal pluralist notion of educational policy directed to the production of a human community sensitive to the many cultural contexts for meaning creation seems to fit well with democratic, egalitarian, pluralist ideals. The power imbalances highlighted by the corporate pluralists, however, point to the implausibility of realizing these ideals until playing fields are leveled. Until then the powerful anglo-conformists in the guise of liberal pluralism, utilizing *human relations* and *teaching the exceptional and culturally different* approaches to education can continue to manipulate the networks of power to get their way. Globally, dwindling resources appear to demand collaborative efforts across cultures if humankind is to survive and prosper while rigid and often archaic political and economic structures combined with ethnocentrism stand in the way.

Ethnocentrisms die hard deaths if they die at all. After seventy years, communism in the former Soviet Union was unable to eradicate them. Educational policies designed to eradicate cultural identities are not likely to be successful either. Anglocentrism must come to be seen as a context for creating reality juxtaposed with other such contexts. Anglos can be proud of their heritage and lionize many aspects of it while at the same time recognizing the contributions made by other groups in the development of the United States. For example, we can be proud of a long Anglo-Saxon tradition of democracy while being sensitive to and equally proud of the contributions of the Iroquois Confederacy to the unique principles upon which our own nation was built. Evidence indicates that prior to contact with Europeans the Five Nations of the Iroquois lived under a constitution that had three main principles: peace, equity or justice, and the power of the "good minds" of the elders over the young.[12] Colonial records show that an Onondaga (one of the Five Nations) named Canassatego suggested that the Colonists form a nation similar to the Iroquois Confederacy during a meeting of the Provincial Council of Pennsylvania in Lancaster on June 25, 1744. The Council members quote Canassatego as telling the Colonists to "receive these your brethren with open arms; unite yourselves to them in the covenant chain and be you with them as one body and one soul."[13] At the Albany Congress between June 19 and July 9, 1754, Benjamin Franklin used the

Iroquois as an example in presenting his own Plan of Union.[14] The Iroquois live under their constitution to this day, but their influence upon the formation of the United States of America is not a widely studied phenomenon in the public schools of the country.

Why aren't these facts common knowledge? And why aren't the contributions of the myriad groups, whose ideas and sweat built our nation, interwoven throughout every subject of every curriculum of every one of our school districts? Why isn't the inquiry process, taught in every classroom, one which views issues and problems through the many faceted prism of cultural heterogeneity with its manifold gradations in hue and perspective? It is for the same reason that the few, all over the globe, rule the many. The many must accept the fictions promulgated by the few. This is our common ideology, the acceptance of a history, a tradition, a conception of reality, of natural order. When ideological commitments are questioned, national unity is threatened, the status quo begins to crumble. The ideology of the ruling elite is anglo-conformity. The role of schooling from this ideological perspective is to assimilate the masses into the anglo-centric mainstream. All people are welcomed into the mainstream as long as they internalize the ideology: its language, rituals, customs, and world-view. This cultural **hegemony** does more to control the behavior of citizens than a ruling military or police force, and it is insidious. It permeates the psyches of individuals. It is an internal, psychological mechanism of control. It raises the specter of the "tyranny of the majority" that Alexis de Tocqueville warned us of in his 1830s tome *Democracy in America,*[15] the tyranny of narrow minds and mean spirits which would crush diversity and compel conformity. de Tocqueville stated, "If ever freedom is lost in America, that will be due to the omnipotence of the majority driving the minorities to desperation and forcing them to appeal to physical force. We may then see anarchy, but it will have come as the result of despotism."[16] The ideology of anglo-conformity when combined with capitalism becomes a nymph, whose siren song is a compelling opiate welcoming all groups into the anglo-centric economic mainstream. When anglo-conformity is inextricably entwined with economic well-being, it carries with it a coercive psychological force which may become enthralling.

But, as our survey has shown, there are a minority of school districts practicing what, in hegemonic terms, may be viewed as a subversive activity called multicultural education. They may not envision their programs in apocalyptic terms, presaging the imminent destruction of anglo-conformity, but, by their actions they confront students with a culturally pluralistic interpretation of reality. They, therefore, suggest to students that they might, at the very least, question the ideological stance of anglo-centrists.

The school districts with multicultural education programs have not adopted a proactive stance which advocates social activism for students, however. Their social goals tend to favor the promotion of social equality and cultural pluralism over the promotion of active social change which will enhance the power position of oppressed peoples. And almost as many of these districts say they want to promote tolerance and acceptance within present society as those who wish to foster multiculturalism. Only ten districts chose the *education that is multicultural and social reconstructionist* position, whereas 101 selected the *multicultural education* goal and eighty-one the *human relations* social objective.

The *education that is multicultural and social reconstructionist* orientation fares somewhat better when it comes to the selection of a school goal. Thirty-five districts with multicultural education programs wish to prepare citizens to work actively toward social equality and promote cultural pluralism, alternative life-styles, and equal opportunity in the school. Many more adopt school goals for the promotion of positive feelings among students, the reduction of stereotyping, and enhancement of students' self-concepts; or, the advancement of equal opportunity in the school, cultural pluralism, respect for those who differ, and support of power equality among groups. The former is a *human relations* school goal for ninety-three districts, whereas the latter, a *multicultural education* school goal, is the choice of ninety-one districts. Twenty-nine districts see their school goal primarily in terms of teaching students to become culturally literate by making the core disciplines relevant to their lives, in Sleeter and Grant terms, a *teaching the exceptional and culturally different* objective. None of the districts responding took a *single-group studies* stance in the selection of a school goal. Thus, fully 49% of the respondents characterize their multicultural education programs' school goals in essentially assimilationist terms.

There is a dramatic shift toward *multicultural education* and *education that is multicultural and social reconstructionist* in the curricular and instructional aims of these districts, however. Although only 123 districts actually report having ethnic studies curricula, a majority of the respondents claim that their curricular aim is to either: (1) teach contributions and perspective of several different groups, critical thinking, analysis of alternative viewpoints; make the curriculum relevant to students' experiential backgrounds; and to promote use of more than one language or dialect (102 districts); or (2) teach current social issues involving racism, classism, sexism, and handicapism; teach experiences and perspectives of several different American groups; use students' life experiences as a starting point for analyzing oppression; and, teach critical thinking, analysis of alternative viewpoints, social action and empowerment (seventy-three districts). This active curricular support of cultural pluralism outstrips by far the assimilationist curricular aims of those supporting *teaching the exceptional and culturally different* (thirty-six districts) and *human relations* (twenty-eight districts) or the *single-group studies* approach adopted by eleven districts.

The instructional aims of the school districts reporting multicultural education programs are even more oriented toward the promotion of cultural pluralism than curricular aims. Eighty-one percent of the districts responding to this survey have adopted *multicultural education* (110 districts) or *education that is multicultural and social reconstructionist* instructional objectives (eighty-eight districts). An examination of the aspects of the classroom incorporated into the multicultural education programs of these districts and the school practices employed bespeaks a broad range of support for cultural pluralism among them. The facts that these districts are a minority of all large school districts in the first place; that the adoption of multicultural approaches to education has trended downward over the past two decades; that even among those districts with multicultural education programs, there is an admixture of assimilationist goals and aims; and, the curricular commitment to ethnic studies has dramatically diminished, must be perceived with alarm by cultural pluralists. For, if our society is to be a culturally pluralistic democracy and demographic trends are toward greater cultural heterogeneity; if we are living more closely together in an electronically, economically, and environmentally symbiotic relationship with our brothers and sisters on a culturally diverse planet; and the demands of citizenship within our nation and world require the abilities to think critically and analytically at high levels of cognitive functioning, to solve problems, to understand one another across cultural divides, and to commit ourselves to our common welfare, how best do we prepare ourselves for the coming challenges facing ourselves, our nation, and our world. And, what is the role of public education in the United States in this endeavor?

Speculative Analysis

For do we have a cultural mortar which, in spite of our heterogeneity, binds us as a nation? What does cultural literacy mean in the midst of diversity? Cultural literacy in our own complex society should not be ethnocentric; it should be metacultural. We can find our national cultural mortar in the mortar of democratic citizenship. All individuals and all groups are invited to participate responsibly in the democratic process. But, it is romantic to think that the social order can be reconstructed through the school alone. The institution of education is not equipped for this task and, if the research reported by Bennett (deMarrais) and Lecompte is correct, the average teacher is a politically conservative "...white, married, woman in her mid-thirties with two children...from a middle to upper-middle class family...likely to teach in a suburban elementary school...comfortable in her rather traditional gender role."[17] This is not the profile of the "educational statesperson" and social activist that reconstructionist George S. Counts envisaged the ideal teacher to be.[18] If we ever are to realize the democratic, egalitarian, pluralistic ideals we nominally espouse and say we cherish, the United States must commit itself to a social compact among its major institutions including education.

This social compact must include a commitment to equity involving the public and private sectors of our nation alike. As we progress toward this ideal a liberally pluralistic multicultural education with a core of democratic studies becomes a focal point of policy reformulation. Democratic studies involve a knowledge base as well as practice in the utilization of democratic methodologies.

Educational policy in the United States should emanate from a core of democratic values. The primary goal of education in our country should be preparation for citizenship in a complex, pluralistic society committed to democratic ideals. Counts felt that "...the highest and most characteristic ethical expression of the genius of the American people is the ideal of democracy"[19] and that educational policy should be based "...on as profound an analysis of social life as [the educator] is capable of making [and] can best be expounded by first examining the relation of education to social action."[20] Pragmatically, an educational policy may be evaluated in terms of the probable social consequences of its application (the "by their fruits ye shall know them" test). In particular, *is the policy likely to lead to democratic outcomes?*[21]

John Dewey has informed us that democracy can be conceived as a philosophicojuristic system. Politically it provides for each citizen being afforded equal legal treatment and the opportunity to participate in the formation of the values which regulate the society. It also offers a set of principles for the conduct of human society permeated with values within political, legal, economic, and socio-cultural contexts. Among these values are included commitments to the individual and social welfare of all persons, the participation of all in a human community of judges, and recognition of individual and minority group rights. Democracy is also associated with an open, flexible, sharable method of science approach to problem solving. Solutions always remain open to amendment if their social consequences are deemed negative. Democratic methodology implies that humans are capable of self-discipline and purposive motivation.

Dewey stated:

> The keynote of democracy as a way of life may be expressed, it seems to me, as the necessity for the participation of every mature human being in formation of values that regulate the living of men together: which is necessary from the standpoint of both the general social welfare and the full development of human beings as individuals.[22]

This growth criterion for democracy is expressed in the following manner by Villemain and Champlin:

> Democracy, reconceived, is that quality of experience which pervades social life, and in so doing contributes to the attainment of the fullest possible growth of all toward qualitative ideals. So defined democracy is a conception about an aesthetic—religious affair.[23]

And, Sidney Hook wrote:

> ...the ultimate commitment of democracy...must be a faith in some method by which...conflicts are resolved. Since the method must be the test of all values, it would not be inaccurate to call it the basic value in the democratic way of life. This method is the method of intelligence, of critical scientific inquiry.[24]

In a review of the writings of recognized scholars of American education and democracy, Byron F. Radebaugh[25] has developed a set of "criterion values" which may be utilized in the formation of educational policies which can be mechanisms for achieving democratic outcomes. Radebaugh was able to glean a core of values that these scholars considered to be basic in the democratic way of life through a content analysis of their works. They felt that knowledge and reflective intelligence, in an environment exemplifying commitments to the Constitutional guarantees of freedom of thought, belief, speech, and press, should be used to promote human welfare on a global basis; that rules for living should be constructed by those to whom they will be applied; that these rules should be judged on the basis of the consequences of their application in terms of the greatest good to the greatest number; that these rules should be tentative and open to amendment if that human community who formulated them deem them to be inadequate; that each citizen should have an equal opportunity to participate in this process; that education in and for a democracy should equip each student with the conceptual wherewithal to participate fully and responsibly in all phases of democratic citizenship; that democratic education be equally accessible to all persons and act as a vehicle for righting imbalances and inequities, be they social, cultural, racial, religious, gender based, political, economic, or otherwise; that intelligence be given free play in solving problems; that avenues for the free expression of minority opinion remain open and exempt from tyranny by the majority; that opinion and the free expression of ideas be held to the tests of evidence and reason; and, that pooled intelligence, consensus, and willingness to abide by mutually agreed upon rules are hallmarks of democracy. From this line of thinking one may discern that education for democracy must be so constructed as to guarantee free, open, and ongoing inquiry into alternative models for thought, as well as the evaluation and reconstruction of those models. Democratic education involves the analysis and improvement of thought and the thought process.

If we, the people of the United States, are to form a more perfect union, in all our heterogeneity, we can not demand adherence to the cultural norms of one group alone. The mechanism which unites us can be our adherence to the democratic method for the solution of our problems. That method, as Sidney Hook instructs us, is the method of critical intelligence. It demands a high level of skill in its use and a high level of commitment among the citizens who adhere to it. It must be taught in schools. It must be imbued deeply in the hearts of the citizens.

Students should, therefore, within the context of a school which thoroughly reflects the cultural pluralism of our nation in its policies, social and school goals, curricular and instructional aims, aspects of the classroom, and school practices, be offered an education which challenges them to attain the highest levels of cognitive functioning of which they are capable and grounds them in democratic theory and process. They should understand democracy in its every aspect. They should study the history of democracies globally and, in particular, American democracy. They should be taught the practice of democratic method in cooperative problem solving endeavors. Schools should accommodate to cultural differences in learning styles. They should practice inclusion across lines of ethnicity, gender, handicap, and social class. They should offer an integrated multidisciplinary, multiethnic, global education curriculum. Students should engage in inquiry which leads them to cooperative humanism and respect for individual and group needs. They should be engendered with the desire and conceptual skills to gather all relevant data; to fully explore alternatives; to use data in arriving at logical conclusions; to judge conclusions reached in light of their possible social consequences; to engage in the reconstruction of systems of judgment; and, ultimately, to be able to use the method of open, sharable, critical inquiry in the absence of the direct guidance of the teacher. A commitment to this democratic method of inquiry—to doubting, questioning, evaluating, reconstructing, to democratic decision-making, and the actualization of human potential are worthy goals for which education may strive. Alternative forms of assessment can be used to measure students' progress in the development of the concepts and skills needed for them to become responsible participants in a culturally pluralistic democracy.

This culturally sensitive education would begin early in the lives of the children of our nation. Early intervention programs such as The Perry Preschool Program of Ypsilante, Michigan have been shown to have long lasting beneficial effects, but have been criticized in some quarters for being culturally genocidal. This early childhood education program, begun in the early 1960s, provided an organized educational experience directed at the intellectual and social development of three and four year-old children. Most stayed in the program for two years. Follow-up studies were conducted on a longitudinal basis, comparing the fifty-eight children who were assigned to the preschool program with a matched control group of sixty-five children who were like the experimental group in every way except that they did not attend the preschool. Over the past thirty years, these 123 African American youths from families of low socioeconomic status who were considered at risk of failing in school have been studied by teams of researchers. The studies address the issue of whether high quality early childhood education would improve the lives of the children, their low-income families, and the life of the community as a whole. Those who participated in the High/Scope Educational Research Foundation's Perry Preschool Program outperformed those who did not. Although, initially, there was not a significant difference in the two groups' academic performance, the Perry preschooler experimental group, to this day, has completed more schooling, committed fewer crimes, had higher rates of employment, and earned higher incomes than those in the control group. Parent outreach and an emphasis on the cognitive development of the children were characteristics of this program.[26]

The Milwaukee Project, conducted by Rick Heber and Howard Garber, is another case in point. Previous research had indicated that there was a connection between the IQ of the mother and the school performance of their offspring. The children of mothers whose IQs were below seventy-five were likely to fail in school, whereas children of mothers whose IQs were above 100 were likely to succeed. In an effort to determine the effects of nature versus nurture, Heber and Garber identified a cohort of African American inner-city women with IQs below seventy-five who had recently given birth. They separated the children into experimental and control groups. The control group was monitored, but that is all. The children in the experimental group, at just a few months of age, were placed in an educational center for most of each day. They received meals there, were placed in a one-to-one relationship with an adult who ministered to their needs, held them, spoke to them, and played with them. Later they were placed in groups of two or three children to one adult. They received early cognitive stimulation, were exposed to a language-oriented curriculum and a highly structured and prescriptive educational environment. Their progress was carefully monitored and what the researchers called a "maternal rehabilitation program" was undertaken. At five years of age the mean IQ of the experimental group was 123.4, significantly higher than the 94.8 average IQ of the control group. None of the experimental group was retarded.

The researchers felt that this was strong evidence for nurture over nature in the cognitive development of young children.[27]

Early childhood education should focus on cognitive development while, at the same time, paying homage to the personal/cultural identities of the children and families involved. As long as diversity is respected in these programs through multicultural education, culturally sensitive early intervention educational programs involving a national system of publicly and privately funded day care would be an important element in a social compact for equity. Desegregation of schools across ethclass lines, heterogeneously grouped classes, and the elimination of tracking and culturally punitive uses of testing would be other elements. Liberally pluralistic multicultural education must be combined with an equitable funding formula for public schools which eliminates the impact of the uneven distribution of wealth in the nation on the quality of education delivered to children of different ethclasses. If we are to equalize educational opportunity for all children, we need to move away from the local property tax as a major source of financial support for public education. It is more reasonable to utilize state and federal income taxes for this purpose. We should combine these funds with funding formulas designed for the production of equity from school district to school district in teacher salaries, class size, school plant, educational materials, and so forth. The driving force in education for all of our children should not be the level of wealth of the communities served by the schools. It should be the maintenance of educational standards of the highest quality for each child no matter what their ethclass or geographic location may be. The role of education in this country must be to provide for each child the most exemplary education we have the capacity to muster. Our survival as a multicultural democracy depends on it.

A revamping of teacher education to the end of adequately preparing a population of teachers equipped to work in an educational system committed to inclusion and multiculturalism, designed to conceptually prepare students for active and responsible participation in a democratic society, is critical. This would include courses with multicultural education content. The program should also be comprised of instruction in methodology for teaching across cultures *and* about diverse peoples. It would entail directed field experience and student teaching in multicultural settings. It should involve contact with teacher education faculty who represent the cultural diversity of the nation. Further, the multicultural education professoriate should work as hard at political action at local, state, and federal levels as they do at furthering their careers by writing articles and books for one another and presenting papers at conferences attended by their peers. For, as Gollnick's research has shown, what governments legislate does have an impact on public school education practice.

These educational policies would be inextricably tied to the development of collaborative economic models on a global basis, a national commitment for equity which would involve workfare and job training and retraining involving public schools, governmental agencies, and the private sector. Ethclass should not be the determining or limiting factor in life chances. For example, in an electronic age all persons need to be computer literate. Access to computers and computer education must not be limited to those who can afford them. The children of low-income families must be prepared through their educational institutions for our new age of communication. It is in the best interests of business, industry, and government to see that each school child is afforded this opportunity. Job creation should be a part of this process as well as a more progressively oriented income tax structure and other reforms. Government can provide incentives through subsidies and tax breaks for industry to develop enterprise zones near low-income areas. Government, industry, and education can work together to provide job training on a mandatory basis for workfare participants. They can also cooperatively provide the early intervention day care opportunities for the children of parents involved in the workfare endeavor and all others who wish to avail themselves of this opportunity for high quality education of young children. There should be a plethora of jobs in the day care facilities alone for certified early childhood educators and teacher aides. Training for these jobs can be carried out, in part, in the day care centers provided by government, industry, and schools. These agencies can also provide training for other jobs in these sectors. As workforce needs change, this cooperative mechanism will be able to adjust by offering retraining and updating experiences to employees and trainees alike.

Preparation for entrepreneurship can also be part of this preparation. Democracy, multiculturalism, and small-scale capitalism are not necessarily incompatible entities, although they are uneasy partners in our continuing experiment in American democracy. Certainly Thomas Jefferson did not envision such an alliance. He developed a mathematically precise scheme for freeing slaves in Virginia which, of course, was not put into practice. It involved educating all slaves born after a legislated date for freedom. At the age of twenty-one for males and eighteen for females, they would be colonized and declared free. Virginia would support the colony until it became self-sufficient at which time it would be severed entirely from dependence on Virginia. During the deportation of the slaves, indentured white servants would be brought in to take their place. The white servants would eventually gain citizenship after the remaining blacks, born before the legislated date, died off in Virginia. Jefferson felt that bringing in indentured servants was the lesser of two evils. In general he opposed large immigrations to Virginia, for he felt that if democracy were to survive the society must retain a certain homogeneity of those who had been brought up under republican forms of government of Western European origin.[28]

If Jefferson did not foresee a culturally pluralistic democracy, Karl Marx and others believed that capitalism and egalitarianism were mutually exclusive. Charles E. Lindblom, in his extraordinary study of the world's political-economic systems[29], points out, however, that "...liberal democracy has arisen only in nations that are market-oriented, not in all of them, but only in them."[30] On the other hand, he goes on to say:

> Enormously large, rich in resources, the big corporations...command more resources than do most government units. They can also, over a broad range, insist that government meet their demands, even if these demands run counter to those of citizens expressed through their **polyarchal** controls. Moreover, they do not disqualify themselves from playing the partisan role of citizen — for the corporation is legally a person and they exercise unusual veto powers. They are on all these counts disproportionately powerful...The large private corporation fits oddly into democratic theory and vision. Indeed, it does not fit.[31]

If government can't provide financial and other inducements to businesses to waive some of their privileges, especially in this age of **oligopolistic** multinational corporations, democracy is faced with a serious dilemma. The democratization of industry through employee ownership and/or participation in corporate policy may be another measure for the production of good corporate citizenship. These problems of democracy should be part and parcel of a multicultural education curriculum for future participants in the democratic experiment called The United States of America.

These reforms would help us realize the ideals of liberal pluralism while remedying the injustices articulated by corporate pluralists. Are we as a nation likely to engage ourselves in such an endeavor? The power elite, in their shortsightedness, probably would not see it in their self-interest to do so. Therefore, we, the combined peoples of the United States, committed to the democratic ideals on which this nation was founded (and will stand) must have the perspicacity and political will to carry it off.

Summary

Although the 1980s was a decade of growth in the development of multicultural educational theory and ethnic studies research, the practice of multicultural education among the largest school districts in the United States declined. Among the 46.1% of these districts which had multicultural education programs in 1995, there was a mix of assimilationist and culturally pluralistic practices. There has been a big drop in the number of ethnic studies curricula since 1974. The curricula which are offered focus on a very few minority groups. The programs available now serve more students and offer more school practices to more grade levels than in 1974, however. There is a definite correlation between government initiatives and the practice of multicultural education. Those states with policies and guidelines for multicultural education have a much higher percentage of school districts with multicultural education programs than those which do not. Although social and school goals for the programs tend to be assimilationist, curricular and instructional aims are multicultural and/or social reconstructionist. Nationally, anglo-conformity predominates.

We are, however, a culturally pluralistic society. If we are to right the social imbalances which exist in our society and are to move toward realization of the pluralist, egalitarian, democratic ideals we nominally espouse and say we cherish as a nation, the United States must commit itself to a social compact among its major institutions including education. This social compact must include a commitment to equality involving the public and private sectors of our nation alike. The public school is not equipped to carry out this task alone, but, for its part, it can offer a liberally pluralistic multicultural education with a core of democratic studies. Each student must emerge from his or her educational experience conceptually and motivationally equipped for full and responsible participation in a culturally pluralistic democracy. A culturally sensitive education of the highest quality should begin early in the lives of the children of our nation. To equalize educational opportunity, an equitable funding formula for public schools which eliminates the impact of the uneven distribution of wealth in the nation on the quality of education delivered to children of different ethclasses should be adopted in combination with: early intervention programs; desegregation of schools across ethclass lines; heterogeneous grouping; culture-fair alternative assessment; inclusion; an integrated multidisciplinary, multiethnic, global education curriculum; instruction sensitive to cultural and gender differences in learning styles; and the revamping of teacher education; among other educational reforms. These school reforms need to be accompanied by the development of collaborative economic models on a global basis, workfare, job training and retraining, a progressive income tax, and the development of cooperative relationships among the public and private sector institutions in our society. Power sharing means the diminution of power in certain, largely anglo-conformist, sectors, however. It is problematic as to whether this is likely to occur, but, at the very least, those committed to democratic cultural pluralism should make the effort.

APPENDIX A

INITIAL SURVEY QUERY LETTER

Dear Colleague:

There has been a lot of discussion being generated of late over what constitutes an adequate public school multicultural education program. Much of the present debate over appropriate forms of education that is multicultural and critiques of multiculturalism in education is weakened by the fact that the contemporary status of multicultural education practice on a national basis is not known.

With your help, I would like to remedy that situation by updating and replicating surveys I conducted in the mid-1970s on grants from the United States Office of Education and other sources. For this year's research I am targeting certain key school districts which should represent the national picture on this issue.

Would you be so kind as to provide me with the information requested on the back of this sheet about the persons to whom I might send a questionnaire within your school district? I would appreciate it if you could also alert those persons to the fact they will be part of a national study of multicultural education. Enclosed please find a postage paid envelope. Please return this to us whether or not you have multicultural education programs so that I will not trouble you again with follow-up mailings.

Thank you very much for responding to this request. The professional service you render by so doing is very much appreciated.

Sincerely,

David E. Washburn, Ph.D.
Professor and Coordinator of Educational Foundations
Department of Curriculum and Foundations
Bloomsburg University of Pennsylvania
(717) 389-4276

continued

Please check appropriate boxe(s):

☐ **No**, we do not have any multicultural education programs.

☐ **Yes**, we have (a) multicultural education program(s).

Program Director (or Contact Person) _____
Title _____
Address _____
_____

Phone Number _____

Program Director (or Contact Person) _____
Title _____
Address _____
_____

Phone Number _____

☐ We have additional multicultural education programs.

Program Director (or Contact Person) _____
Title _____
Address _____
_____

Phone Number _____

Program Director (or Contact Person) _____
Title _____
Address _____
_____

Phone Number _____

Program Director (or Contact Person) _____
Title _____
Address _____
_____

Phone Number _____

APPENDIX B

SURVEY FOLLOW-UP LETTER

Dear Colleague:

A few weeks ago I sent you the enclosed letter. On the back of the letter you were asked to check the *no* box if you have no multicultural education program within your school district and the *yes* box if you do.

I am surveying the 713 largest school districts in the United States. Since your school district is one of the 713, I would appreciate it if you would take just a few minutes to complete the form so that the statistics will be accurate.

Please respond utilizing the postage paid envelope accompanying this letter. Thank you for your assistance.

Sincerely,

David E. Washburn, Ph.D.
Professor and Coordinator of Educational Foundations
Department of Curriculum and Foundations
Bloomsburg University of Pennsylvania
(717) 389-4276

Appendix C

Survey Cover Letter

Dear Colleague:

Your superintendent has identified you as a director of a multicultural education program in your district and as a person willing to participate in a national study of multicultural education. As you know, there has been much discussion of late over what constitutes an adequate public school multicultural education program. However, the contemporary status of multicultural education practice on a national basis is unknown.

With your help, I would like to remedy that situation by updating and replicating surveys I conducted in the mid-1970s on grants from The United States Office of Education and other sources. I am surveying the 713 largest school districts in the United States.

Please be so kind as to complete the enclosed questionnaire and return it in the postage paid envelope provided. I will inform you of the results of this survey which should give us a picture of the contemporary status of multicultural education in the Untied States.

Thank you very much for responding to this request. The professional service you render by so doing is very much appreciated.

Sincerely,

David E. Washburn, Ph.D.
Professor and Coordinator of Educational Foundations
Department of Curriculum and Foundations
Bloomsburg University of Pennsylvania
(717) 389-4276

APPENDIX D

THE 1995 MULTICULTURAL EDUCATION SURVEY INSTRUMENT

Multicultural Education Survey

Name_____
Title_____
Address_____
_____
Phone Number_____
School District_____
Program Name_____

Please answer the following questions.

1. How long has your multicultural education program been in operation?
   _____ years

2. Which grade levels are involved in your program? (please check all appropriate boxes)
   ☐K ☐1 ☐2 ☐3 ☐4 ☐5 ☐6 ☐7 ☐8 ☐9 ☐10 ☐11 ☐12

3. How many students participate in your program per academic school year?
   _____ students

4. What is the ethnic composition of your student population? (percentages)
   _____ % African American
   _____ % Asian/Pacific Islander American
   _____ % European American (White, Non-Hispanic)
   _____ % Hispanic (Latino/Chicano) American
   _____ % Native American
   _____ % Other

5. What is the ethnic composition of your full-time staff? (percentages)

   Administrative
   _____ % African American
   _____ % Asian/Pacific Islander American
   _____ % European American (White, Non-Hispanic)
   _____ % Hispanic (Latino/Chicano) American
   _____ % Native American
   _____ % Other

continued

5. (continued)

Instructional
_____ % African American
_____ % Asian/Pacific Islander American
_____ % European American (White, Non-Hispanic)
_____ % Hispanic (Latino/Chicano) American
_____ % Native American
_____ % Other

Support
_____ % African American
_____ % Asian/Pacific Islander American
_____ % European American (White, Non-Hispanic)
_____ % Hispanic (Latino/Chicano) American
_____ % Native American
_____ % Other

6. Is there community involvement in your program?
☐ yes   ☐ no

If yes, of what type? (check all that apply)
_____ community involvement in curriculum planning
_____ use of community resources
_____ use of human resources in the community
_____ a community-based instructional program
_____ study of the community
_____ interaction with community organizations
_____ other(s) (please specify)

_____
_____
_____
_____

*For the following five questions, please restrict your answer to **one** response.*

7. Which *one* of the following comes closest to characterizing the *social goal* of your multicultural education program?

_____ help students fit into present society
_____ promote tolerance and acceptance within present society
_____ promote equality and recognition of a particular group or groups
_____ promote social equality and cultural pluralism
_____ promote active change which will enhance the power position of oppressed peoples

8. Which *one* of the following comes closest to characterizing the *school goals* of your multicultural education program?

_____ teach students to become culturally literate by making the core disciplines relevant to their lives

_____ promote positive feelings among students, reduce stereotyping, promote students' self-concepts

_____ develop in students the motivation and knowledge to work toward social change that would benefit their particular group

_____ promote equal opportunity in the school, cultural pluralism, respect for those who differ, and support of power equality among groups

_____ prepare citizens to work actively toward social equality; promote cultural pluralism and alternative lifestyles; promote equal opportunity in the school

9. Which *one* of the following is the primary *target population* of your multicultural education program?

_____ low achieving students

_____ minority students

_____ all students

10. Which *one* set of practice comes closest to characterizing the *curricular aims* of your multicultural education program?

_____ make the curriculum relevant to students' experiential background; fill in gaps in basic skills and knowledge

_____ teach lessons about stereotyping, name-calling, individual differences and similarities, and contributions of groups of which students are members

_____ teach units or courses about the culture of a group, how the group has been victimized, current social issues facing the group—from the perspective of that group

_____ teach contributions and perspectives of several different groups, critical thinking, analyses of alternative viewpoints; make curriculum relevant to students' experiential backgrounds; promote use of more than one language or dialect

_____ teach current social issues involving racism, classism, sexism, handicapism; teach experiences and perspectives of several different American groups; use students' life experiences as a starting point for analyzing oppression; teach critical thinking, analysis of alternative viewpoints, social action and empowerment

11. Which *one* of the following comes closest to characterizing the *instructional aims* of your multicultural education program?

_____ build on students' learning styles; adapt to students' skill levels; teach as
         effectively and efficiently as possible to enable students to catch up
_____ use cooperative learning; use real or vicarious experiences with others
_____ build on the learning styles of the students' groups
_____ build on the students' learning styles; adapt to the students' skill levels;
         involve students actively in thinking and analyzing; use cooperative
         learning
_____ involve students actively in democratic decision making; build on students'
         learning styles; adapt to students' skill levels; use cooperative learning;
         develop a spirit of social activism

*For the following five questions, check **all** responses that apply.*

12. Which of the following *aspects of the classroom* are incorporated into your multicultural education program?

_____ use decorations showing group members integrated into mainstream of
         society
_____ decorate classroom to reflect uniqueness and accomplishments of students;
         decorate in "I'm okay, you're okay" themes
_____ use decorations reflecting cultural and classroom contributions of a
         particular group; have representatives of a particular group involved in
         class (e.g. as guest speakers)
_____ decorate classroom to reflect cultural pluralism, nontraditional sex roles,
         disabled people, and student interests
_____ decorate classroom to reflect social action themes, cultural diversity, student
         interests, and aspects of society that need to be changed in order to achieve
         equal justice for all

13. Which of the following *school practices* are incorporated into your multicultural education program?

_____ transitional bilingual education
_____ English as a second language
_____ remedial classes
_____ special education as temporary and intensive aids to fill gaps in knowledge
_____ involve lower-class and minority parents in supporting work of the school
_____ activities and school policies and practices which do not "put down" or leave out some groups of students
_____ school-wide activities, such as donating food for the poor, aimed at peace and unity
_____ employ faculty who are members of the group or groups being studied
_____ involve lower-class and minority parents in decisions concerning school policies and practices
_____ staffing pattern includes diverse racial, gender, and disability groups in non-traditional roles
_____ use decorations, special events, and school menus which reflect and include diverse groups
_____ use of library materials which portray groups in diverse roles
_____ include all student groups in extra-curricular activities
_____ discipline procedures do not penalize any particular group
_____ school buildings are accessible to disabled people
_____ student involvement in democratic decision making about substantive school-wide concerns
_____ school involved in local community action projects
_____ human relations training for teachers
_____ community involvement in school policy decisions
_____ a strong school-community public relations effort
_____ inservice teacher training in multicultural education
_____ student involvement in curriculum planning
_____ instruction in Spanish as a second language
_____ student involvement in school policy decisions
_____ an inter-racial student council
_____ human relations training for students
_____ a professionally staffed community relations office
_____ a bilingual curriculum
_____ a professionally staffed human relations team
_____ a student human relations council
_____ a bicultural curriculum
_____ a multilingual curriculum
_____ instruction in standard English as a second dialect
_____ instruction in Asian language(s) as second language(s)
_____ instruction in Native American language(s) as second language(s)
_____ an ethnic studies curriculum

14. If you have an *ethnic studies curriculum*, does it include the study of groups which could be included under the following general categories? If so, which ones?

_____ African Americans   _____ Irish Americans
_____ Arab Americans   _____ Italian Americans
_____ Asian/Pacific Islander Americans   _____ Native Americans
_____ French Americans   _____ Portuguese Americans
_____ German Americans   _____ Scandinavian Americans
_____ Greek Americans   _____ Slavic Americans
_____ Hispanic (Latino/Chicano) Americans _____ Other(s) (please specify)
_____ Iranian Americans

_____

_____

15. Which *disciplines* participate in your ethnic studies curriculum?

_____ Art   _____ Language Arts
_____ Business   _____ Mathematics
_____ English   _____ Music
_____ Foreign Languages   _____ Physical Education
_____ Health   _____ Reading
_____ Home Economics   _____ Science
_____ Humanities   _____ Social Sciences
_____ Industrial Arts   _____ Theater
                           _____ Other(s) (please specify)

_____

_____

16. What *elements* concerning the groups which you study are included in your curriculum?

_____ Art   _____ Literature
_____ Attitudes   _____ Material Culture
_____ Beliefs   _____ Music
_____ Body Language   _____ Physical Characteristics
_____ Culture and Personality _____ Religion
_____ Dialect   _____ Social Customs
_____ Drama   _____ Social Organization
_____ Foods   _____ Social Structure
_____ History   _____ Values
_____ Kinship Structure   _____ Other(s) (please specify)
_____ Language

_____

_____

17.   Has your school produced materials for use in your program?

_____ yes   _____ no

18.   If yes, are any available for purchase?

_____ yes   _____ no

If possible, please send lists of materials available for purchase and copies of any other locally produced materials. Units, course outlines, syllabi, curriculum guides, bibliographies, course catalogues, program descriptions, etc. are most welcome and appreciated. Thank you.

Additional comments (please write below)

Thank you very much for your time and participation.

NOTES

INTRODUCTION A Conceptual Framework for Multicultural Education

1. Adapted from David E. Washburn, "A Conceptual Framework for Multicultural Education," *The Florida FL Reporter*, 10, 1 and 2 (Spring/Fall 1972): 27.

CHAPTER ONE Muticultural Education: Origins, Development, and Prospects

1. Adapted from David E. Washburn, "Multicultural Education: Origins, Development and Prospects," *Research Bulletin* Florida Agricultural and Mechanical University 23, 1 (May 1979): 33-39.
2. William Greenbaum, "America in Search of a New Ideal: An Essay on the Rise of Pluralism," *Harvard Educational Review* 44, 3 (August 1974): 434-435.
3. See David E. Washburn, *Ethnic Studies in Pennsylvania* (Pittsburgh: University of Pittsburgh Center for International Studies, 1978).
4. Horace M. Kallen, *Cultural Pluralism and the American Idea* (Philadelphia: University of Pennsylvania Press, 1956).
5. Michael Harrington, *The Other America* (Baltimore: Penguin Books, Inc., 1971).
6. See David E. Washburn, *Democracy and the Education of the Disadvantaged: A Pragmatic Inquiry* (Portland, Oregon: Lewis and Clark College, 1971).
7. Oscar Lewis, *The Children of Sanchez: Autobiography of a Mexican Family* (New York: Random House, 1961).
8. John H. Chilcott, "An Analysis of the Enculturation of Values as Illustrated in Primary Readers 1879-1960" (paper presented at the California Educational Research Association Meeting, Palo Alto, Calif., March 4, 1961).
9. Raymond H. Giles and Donna M. Gollnick, "Ethnic/Cultural Diversity As Reflected in Federal and State Educational Legislation and Policies," in *Pluralism and the American Teacher: Issues and Case Studies*, ed. Frank H. Klassen and Donna M. Gollnick, 115-160 (Washington, D.C.: Ethnic Heritage Center for Teacher Education of the American Association of Colleges for Teacher Education, 1977).
10. David E. Washburn, *Multicultural Education Programs, Ethnic Studies Curricula, and Ethnic Studies Materials in the United States Public Schools* (Washington, D.C.: ERIC Clearinghouse on Teacher Education, 1980).
11. David E. Washburn, "Multicultural Education in the United States," *Phi Delta Kappan* 56, 9 (May 1975): 636.
12. *Ibid.*
13. David E. Washburn, "Ethnic Studies in the United States," *Educational Leadership* 32, 6 (March, 1975): 409-412.
14. David E. Washburn, "The Pennsylvania Ethnic Heritage Studies Survey," *Pennsylvania Ethnic Studies Newsletter* 3, 1 (September 1977): 3-7.
15. Raymond H. Giles and Donna M. Gollnick, "Ethnic/Cultural Diversity As Reflected in Federal and State Educational Legislation and Policies," 135.
16. Pennsylvania (Commonwealth of), *Senate Bill No. 1618*, 1974, Act No. 322: 872.

17. Raymond H. Giles and Donna M. Gollnick, "Ethnic/Cultural Diversity As Reflected in Federal and State Educational Legislation and Policies," 137.

18. *Ibid.*, 152.

19. David E. Washburn, "Where to Find Ethnic Studies Materials," *Social Education* 39, 1 (January 1975): 40-41.

20. E.g. see Donna M. Gollnick, Frank H. Klassen, and Joost Yff, *Multicultural Education and Ethnic Studies in the United States: An Analysis and Annotated Bibliography of Selected Documents in ERIC* (Washington, D.C.: American Association of Colleges for Teacher Education, 1976); Elizabeth S. Haller, *New Perspectives: A Bibliography of Racial, Ethnic, and Feminist Resources* (Harrisburg: Pennsylvania Department of Education, 1977); *Materials and Human Resources for Teaching Ethnic Studies* (Boulder: Social Science Education Consortium, Inc., 1975); David E. Washburn, *The Peoples of Pennsylvania: An Annotated Bibliography of Resource Materials* (Pittsburgh: University of Pittsburgh Center for International Studies, 1981); David E. Washburn, *Multicultural Education: A Chronological Bibliography of Selected Materials* (Washington, D.C.: ERIC Clearinghouse on Teacher Education, 1981).

21. E.g. see David E. Washburn, *Directory of Ethnic Studies in Pennsylvania* (Pittsburgh: University of Pittsburgh Center for International Studies, 1978) and *Ethnic Studies, Bilingual/Bicultural Education and Multicultural Teacher Education: A Directory of Higher Education Programs and Personnel* (Miami: Inquiry International, 1979).

22. Elizabeth Farquhar, "Title IX: The Ethnic Heritage Studies Program—The 'What' and 'How To'," *Momentum* 6 (October 1975): 46-50.

23. See *Black Studies in Schools* (Arlington: National School Public Relations Association, 1970); William A. Hunter ed., *Multicultural Education Through Competency Based Teacher Education* (Washington, D.C.: American Association of Colleges for Teacher Education, 1974); Fern Kelly, "A System Approaches Multicultural Education," *Educational Leadership* 32 (December 1974): 183-186; *Providing K-12 Multi-Cultural Curricular Experiences* (Columbus: Office of Equal Educational Opportunity, Ohio Department of Education, 1974).

24. David E. Washburn, "Ethnic Studies in the United States," 411.

25. *American Association of School Administrators 1976 Platform* (Arlington: American Association of School Administrators, 1976): William A. Hunter ed., *Multicultural Education Through Competency Based Teacher Education*; James A. Banks et. al. *Curriculum Guidelines for Multiethnic Education: Position Statement* (Arlington: National Council for the Social Studies, 1976); James B. MacDonald, Cultural Pluralism as ASCD's Major Thrust," *Educational Leadership*, 32 (December 1974): 167; *National Association of Elementary School Principals 1975 Platform* (Arlington: National Association of Elementary School Principals, 1975); *1975 Policy Statements of the Council of Chief State School Officers* (Washington, D.C.: Council of Chief State School Officers, 1975); *Secondary Schools in a Changing Society. This We Believe* (Reston: National Association of Secondary School Principals, 1975).

26. David E. Washburn, "Multicultural Education: Origins, Development and Prospects," 38.

27. Chris Raymond, "Global Migration Will Have Widespread Impact on Society, Scholars Say," *The Chronicle of Higher Education* (September 12, 1990): A-1,6.

CHAPTER TWO Multicultural Education: Conceptions and Descriptions

1. David E. Washburn, "Where to Find Ethnic Studies Materials," *Social Education* 39, 1 (January 1975): 40-41; "The Pennsylvania Ethnic Heritage Studies Survey," *Pennsylvania Ethnic Studies Newsletter* 3, 1 (September 1977): 3-7: "Multiethnic Education in Pennsylvania," *Phi Delta Kappan* 59, 8 (April 1978): 561; *Ethnic Studies in Pennsylvania* (Pittsburgh: University of Pittsburgh Center for International Studies, 1978); *Directory of Ethnic Studies in Pennsylvania* (Pittsburgh: University of Pittsburgh Center for International Studies, 1978); *Ethnic Studies, Bilingual/Bicultural Education and Multicultural Teacher Education in the United States: A Directory of Higher Education Programs and Personnel* (Miami: Inquiry International, 1979); *Multicultural Education Programs, Ethnic Studies Curricula, and Ethnic Studies Materials in the United States Public Schools* (Washington, D.C.: Educational Resources Information Center Clearinghouse on Teacher Education, 1980); *Bilingual/Bicultural Education in the United States: Higher Education* (Washington, D.C.: Educational Resources Information Center Clearinghouse on Teacher Education, 1981); *Multicultural Teacher Education in the United States* (Washington, D.C.: Educational Resources Information Center Clearinghouse on Teacher Education, 1981); *Ethnic Studies in the United States: Higher Education* (Washington, D.C.: Educational Resources Information Center Clearinghouse on Higher Education, 1981); "Cultural Pluralism: Are Teachers Prepared?" *Phi Delta Kappan* 63, 7 (March 1982): 493-495; and "Ethnic Studies in the United States: Higher Education," *CORE: An International Journal of Educational Research*, Carfax Publishing Company, Oxford, England 6, 3 (1982): Fiche 15 G8.

2. Christine E. Sleeter and Carl A. Grant, *Making Choices for Multicultural Education: Five Approaches to Race, Class, and Gender* (Columbus: Merril Publishing Company, 1988).

3. *Ibid.*, 14-26.

4. *Ibid.*, 67.

5. *Ibid.*, 100.

6. *Ibid.*, 131.

7. *Ibid.*, 168-169.

8. *Ibid.*, 201.

9. See Milton M. Gordon, *Assimilation in American Life* (New York: Oxford University Press, 1964) and *Human Nature, Class, and Ethnicity* (New York: Oxford University Press, 1978).

10. Milton M. Gordon, *Assimilation in American Life*, 85.

11. *Ibid.*, 51-53.

12. *Ibid.*, 111.

13. *Public Broadcasting System*, "Firing Line Special Debate—Resolved: Freedom of Thought is in Danger on American Campuses," produced by Warren Steibel in association with South Carolina Instructional Television (September 6, 1991).

14. John Silber, *Straight Shooting: What's Wrong With America and How to Fix It* (New York: Harper and Row, 1989).

15. Allan Bloom, *The Closing of the American Mind* (New York: Simon and Schuster, 1987).

16. E. D. Hirsch, Jr., *Cultural Literacy: What Every American Needs to Know* (Boston: Houghton Mifflin Company, 1987); *The Dictionary of Cultural Literacy: What Every American Needs to Know* (Boston: Houghton Mifflin Company, 1988); and, *A First Dictionary of Cultural Literacy* (Boston: Houghton Mifflin Company, 1989).

17. William J. Bennett, *Our Children and Our Country: Improving America's Schools and Affirming the Common Culture* (New York: Simon and Schuster, 1988).

18. Lynne V. Cheney, *American Memory: A Report on the Humanities in the Nation's Public Schools* (Washington, D.C.: National Endowment for the Humanities, 1987); and, *Tyrannical Machines: A Report on Educational Practices Gone Wrong and Our Best Hopes for Setting Them Straight* (Washington, D.C.: National Endowment for the Humanities, 1990).

19. Dinesh D'Souza, *Illiberal Education: The Policies of Race and Sex on Campus* (New York: The Free Press, 1991).

20. Horace M. Kallen, *Culture and Democracy in The United States* (New York: Boni and Liveright, 1924. Reprint Edition 1970 by Arno Press, Inc.).

21. John Dewey, "Nationalizing Education," *Addresses and Proceedings of the Fifty-Fourth Annual Meeting* (National Education Association of The United States, 1916): 185-186.

22. William E. Vickery and Stewart G. Cole, *Intercultural Education in American Schools* (New York and London: Harper and Brothers, 1943); Stewart Cole and Mildred Wiese Cole, *Minorities and the American Promise* (New York: Harper and Brothers, 1954).

23. For example see James A. Banks, *Teaching Ethnic Studies: Concepts and Strategies*, 43rd yearbook (Washington, D.C.: National Council for the Social Studies, 1973); James A. Banks, *Teaching Strategies for Ethnic Studies*, Fifth Edition (Boston: Allyn and Bacon, 1991); James A. Banks, "Approaches to Multicultural Curriculum Reform," in J. A. Banks and C. A. M. Banks, eds., *Multicultural Education: Issues and Perspectives*, second edition (Boston: Allyn and Bacon, 1993), 195-214; James A. Banks, *Multiethnic Education: Theory and Practice*, third edition (Boston: Allyn and Bacon, 1994); James A. Banks, *An Introduction to Multicultural Education* (Boston: Allyn and Bacon, 1994).

24. Hundreds of articles and many books have been written from this point of view. For example, see David E. Washburn, *Multicultural Education: A Chronological Bibliography of Selected Materials* (Washington, D.C.: Educational Resources Information Center Clearinghouse on Teacher Education, 1981). Also see: Donna M. Gollnick and Philip C. Chinn, *Multicultural Education in a Pluralistic Society* (Columbus: Merril Publishing Company, 1990); Carl A. Grant, ed., *Educating for Diversity: An Anthology of Multicultural Voices* (Boston: Allyn and Bacon, 1995); Sonia Nieto, *Affirming Diversity: The Sociopolitical Context of Multicultural Education*, second edition (New York: Longman, 1996); Joel Spring, *Deculturalization and the Struggle for Equality: A Brief History of the Education of Dominated Cultures in the United States* (New York: McGraw-Hill, Inc., 1994),

and *The Intersection of Cultures: Multicultural Education in the United States* (New York: McGraw-Hill, Inc., 1995).

25. James A. Banks, "Multicultural Education: Characteristics and Goals," in *Multicultural Education: Issues and Perspectives*, second edition, eds. James A. Banks and Cherry A.McGee Banks, (Boston: Allyn and Bacon, 1993), 3.

26. See James A. Banks, *Teaching Strategies for Ethnic Studies.*

27. Milton M. Gordon, *Human Nature, Class, and Ethnicity*, 87-89.

28. David E. Washburn, "A Conceptual Framework for Multicultural Education," *The Florida FL Reporter* 10 (Spring/Fall 1972): 27-28.

29. *Ibid.*

30. See James A. Anderson, "Cognitive Styles and Multicultural Populations," *Journal of Teacher Education* 39, 1 (January-February 1988): 2-9; James A. Anderson, "Reaching Beyond Monoculturalism: Acknowledging the Demands of Diversity," *SAEOPP Journal* 8, 2 (1989).

31. Gordon, *Human Nature, Class, and Ethnicity*, 87-89.

32. For example, see J. Cummins, "Empowering Minority Students: A Framework For Intervention," *Harvard Educational Review* 56 (Spring 1986): 18-36; H. Giroux, *Theory and Resistance In Education: A Pedagogy For the Opposition* (South Hadley, Massachusetts: Bergin and Garvey, 1983); "Critical Pedagogy, Cultural Politics and the Discourse of Experience," *Journal of Education*, 167,1 (1985): 22-41; and, "Literacy and the Pedagogy of Voice and Political Empowerment," *Educational Theory* 38 (1988): 61-75; C. McCarthy, "Race and Education in The United States: The Multicultural Solution,"*Interchange* 21 (1990): 45-55; and, *Race and Curriculum: Social Inequality and the Theories and Politics of Difference in Contemporary Research on Schooling* (London: The Falmer Press, 1990); P. McLaren, *Life in Schools: An Introduction to Critical Pedagogy in the Foundations of Education* (New York: Longman, 1989); M. Olneck, "The Recurring Dream: Symbolism and Ideology in Intercultural and Multicultural Education," *American Journal of Education* 98, 2 (1989): 147-174; M. Sarup, *The Politics of Multiracial Education* (New York: Routledge and Kegan Paul, 1986); Christine E. Sleeter, *Empowerment Through Multicultural Education* (Albany: State University of New York Press, 1991).

33. See "A School for Black Males: Is It An Answer for Baltimore?" *The Abell Report* 2, 5 (January/February 1991): 1-4; C. R. Gibbs, "Project 2000: Why Black Men Should Teach Black Boys," *Dollars and Sense* (February/March 1991): 19-27; Spencer Holland et. al., *Project 2000* (Baltimore: Center For Educating African-American Males, Morgan State University's School of Education and Urban Studies, 1990); William Oliver, "Black Males and Social Problems: Prevention Through Afrocentric Socialization," *Journal of Black Studies* 19 (September 1989): 15-39.

34. David E. Washburn, "Multicultural Education in the United States" (1975); "Where to Find Ethnic Studies Materials" (1975); "Ethnic Studies in the United States" (1975); "The Pennsylvania Ethnic Heritage Studies Survey" (1972); "Multiethnic Education in Pennsylvania" (1978); *Ethnic Studies in Pennsylvania* (1978); *Multicultural Education Programs, Ethnic Studies Curricula, and Ethnic Studies Materials in the United States Public Schools* (1980); *Bilingual/Bicultural Education in the United States: Higher Education* (1981); *Multicultural Teacher*

Education in the United States (1981); *Ethnic Studies in the United States: Higher Education* (1981); "Cultural Pluralism: Are Teachers Prepared?" (1982); and, "Ethnic Studies in the United States: Higher Education" (1982).

35. See Gwendolyn C. Baker, "Multicultural Training for Student Teachers," *Journal of Teacher Education* (Winter 1973): 306,307; Ella M. Bowen and Frederick L. Salsman, "Integrating Multiculturalism into a Teacher Training Program," *Journal of Negro Education* (Summer 1979): 390-395, and "Internship in Integration," *Nation's Schools and Colleges* (March 1975): 30, 31; Marjorie E. Sowers, "Opportunity Week: Increasing Multicultural Awareness in a Teacher Education Program," *Teacher Educator* (Summer 1979): 32-36.

36. Murry Nelson, "Ethnic Studies Programs—Some Historical Antecedents," *Social Studies* 68, 3 (1977): 104-108.

37. Richard Gambino, *A Guide to Ethnic Studies Programs in American Colleges, Universities and Schools* (New York: The Rockefeller Foundation Working Papers, 1975).

38. Lawrence J. McConville, *Ethnic Studies Curricula and Related Institutional Entities at Southwestern Colleges and Universities* (El Paso: The Cross-Cultural Southwest Ethnic Study Center, The University of Texas at El Paso, 1975).

39. Winnie Bengelsdorf, *Ethnic Studies in Higher Education: State of the Art and Bibliography* (Washington, D.C.: American Association of State Colleges and Universities, 1972).

40. For example, see R. Caselli, "Ethnic Studies—Opportunity to Revitalize Education" *Contemporary Education* 42, 6 (1971): 301-304; Anthony Clarke, "Ethnic Studies: Reflection and Re-Examination," *Journal of Negro Education* 46, 2 (1977): 124-132; Lawrence P. Crouchett, "The Merger of Ethnic Studies and General Education," *The Journal of Ethnic Studies* 6, 2 (1978): 35-48; Jane Casssels Record and Wilson Record, "Ethnic Studies and Affirmative Action—Ideological Roots and Implications for Quality of American Life," *Social Science Quarterly* 55, 2 (1974): 502-519.

41. See James A. Banks, *Teaching Strategies for Ethnic Studies*, second edition (1979: Boston, Allyn and Bacon, Inc.); Karl B. Bonutti, "Ethnic Studies—Another Experiment or Just a Belated Beginning?" *Momentum* 6, 3 (1975): 41-45; Victor Greene, "Old Ethnic Stereotypes and the New Ethnic Studies," *Ethnicity* 5, 4 (1978): 328-350; David E. Washburn, *Ethnic Studies in Pennsylvania* (Pittsburgh: University of Pittsburgh Center for International Studies, 1978).

42. Pierre L. van den Berghe, "The Present State of Comparative Race and Ethnic Studies," *Problems in International Comparative Research in the Social Sciences*, eds. Jan Berting, Felix Geyer and Ray Jurkovich, (New York: Pergamon Press, 1979): 23-36.

43. Gambino, *A Guide to Ethnic Studies Programs*, 14.

44. Record and Record, "Ethnic Studies and Affirmative Action," 507.

45. *Ibid.*, 511.

46. See James A. Banks, *Teaching Ethnic Studies: Concepts and Strategies* (Washington, D.C.: National Council for the Social Studies 43rd Yearbook, 1973); see Banks, *Teaching Strategies for Ethnic Studies*; Bonutti, "Ethnic Studies—Another Experiment or Just a Belated Beginning?," 41-45; Carlos Cortes with Fay Metcalf and Sherryl Hawke, *Understanding You and Them: Tips for Teaching About*

Ethnicity (Boulder: Social Science Education Consortium, Inc., 1976); Richard Gambino, *A Guide to Ethnic Studies Programs in American Colleges, Universities and Schools*; Victor Greene, "Old Ethnic Stereotypes and the New Ethnic Studies,"; Mark M. Krug, "Teaching the Experience of White Ethnic Groups," in *Teaching Ethnic Studies: Concepts and Strategies*, ed. James A. Banks (Washington, D.C.: National Council for the Social Studies 43rd Yearbook; 1973): 257-277; R. P. Swiereng, "Ethnocultural Political Analysis—New Approach to American Ethnic Studies," *Journal of American Studies* 5, 1 (1971): 59-79; Pierre L. van den Berghe, "The Present State of Comparative Race and Ethnic Studies"; David E. Washburn, *Ethnic Studies in Pennsylvania*.

47. See James A. Banks *Teaching Ethnic Studies: Concepts and Strategies*; see Banks *Teaching Strategies for Ethnic Studies*; Carlos Cortes, *Understanding You and Them: Tips for Teaching about Ethnicity*; Shirley Kolack, "A Course in Ethnic Studies," *Teaching Sociology* 3, 1 (1975): 60-73; Bryan Thompson and Carol Agocs, "Ethnic Studies: Teaching and Research Needs" *Journal of Geography* 72 (1973): 13-23; David E. Washburn, "Ethnic Studies in the United States," *Educational Leadership*; David E. Washburn, *Ethnic Studies in Pennsylvania*.

48. Donna M. Gollnick, "National and State Initiatives for Multicultural Education," in *Handbook of Research on Multicultural Education*, eds. James A. Banks and Cherry A. McGee Banks (New York: Simon and Schuster Macmillan, 1995), 44-64.

49. *Ibid.*, 61.

50. *Ibid.*, 61.

51. *Ibid.*, 58.

CHAPTER THREE The 1995 Multicultural Education Survey

1. David E. Washburn, *Multicultural Education Programs, Ethnic Studies Curricula, and Ethnic Studies Materials in the United States Public Schools*.

2. United States Department of Education, *Directory of Public Elementary and Secondary Education Agencies: 1992-93* (Washington, D.C.: National Center for Education Statistics, 1994).

3. Christine E. Sleeter and Carl A. Grant, *Making Choices for Multicultural Education*.

CHAPTER FOUR The Status of Multicultural Education in the United States

1. For information concerning the purchase of multicultural education materials produced by school districts as well as a complete description of each multicultural education program in the United States see, David E. Washburn and Neil L. Brown, *The Multicultural Education Directory* (Philadelphia: Inquiry International, 1996).

2. Christine E. Sleeter and Carl A. Grant, *Making Choices for Multicultural Education*.

CHAPTER FIVE Reconceptualizing Multicultural Education for the Twenty-First Century

1. Portions of this chapter are adapted from: David E. Washburn, "Reinventing the Social Foundations of Education," *Educational Foundations* 7, 4 (Fall 1993): 71-

76; "Let's Take A Hard Look at Multicultural Education," *Multicultural Education* 2, 2 (Winter 1994): 20-23; *A Social Foundations Approach to Educational Policy Analysis* (Eugene, Oregon: Educational Resources Information Center Clearinghouse on Educational Management, 1995); and *Multicultural Education Policy in the United States: A Social Foundations Analysis* (Eugene, Oregon: Educational Resources Information Center Clearinghouse on Educational Management, 1995).

2. David E. Washburn and Neil L. Brown, *The Multicultural Education Directory*.

3. James A. Banks, "Multicultural Education: Historical Development, Dimensions, and Practice," in *Handbook of Research on Multicultural Education*, eds. James A. Banks and Cherry A. McGee Banks (New York: Simon and Schuster Macmillan, 1995), 11.

4. Donna M. Gollnick, "National and State Initiatives for Multicultural Education," 45.

5. *Ibid.*, 48.

6. *Ibid.*, 53.

7. *Ibid.*, 54.

8. *Ibid.*, 55.

9. *Ibid.*, 52-53.

10. Christine E. Sleeter and Carl A. Grant, *Making Choices for Multicultural Education*.

11. Milton M. Gordon, *Assimilation in American Life*; and, *Human Nature, Class, and Ethnicity*.

12. "Iroquois Constitution: A Forerunner to Colonists' Democratic Principles," *New York Times* (June 28, 1987): 40.

13. *Ibid.*

14. *Ibid.*

15. Alexis de Tocqueville, *Democracy in America*, J. P. Mayer and Max Lerner, eds., George Laurence, trans. (New York: Harper and Row, 1966).

16. *Ibid.*, 240.

17. Kathleen P. Bennett and Margaret D. Lecompte, *How Schools Work: A Sociological Analysis of Education* (New York: Longman, 1990): 129-130.

18. George S. Counts, *The Social Foundations of Education* (New York: Charles Scribner's Sons, 1934).

19. *Ibid.*, 9.

20. *Ibid.*, 532-533.

21. For a discussion of education as a distinctive discipline for democracy see, Ephraim Vern Sayers and Ward Madden, *Education and the Democratic Faith* (New York: Appleton, Century-Crofts, Inc., 1959). For an illustrative analysis of educational policy from this frame of reference see, David E. Washburn, *Democracy and the Education of the Disadvantaged: A Pragmatic Inquiry* (Portland, Oregon: Lewis and Clark College, 1971).

22. Joseph Rather, ed., *Intelligence in the Modern World: John Dewey's Philosophy* (New York: Random House, 1939), 400.

23. Francis T. Villemain and Nathaniel Champlin, "Frontiers for an Experimentalist Philosophy of Education," in *Readings in Art Education*, eds. Elliot W. Eisner and David W. Ecker (Waltham: Blausdell Publishing Company, 1966), 453.

24. Sidney Hook, *Reason, Social Myths and Democracy* (New York: The John Day Company, 1940), 295.

25. Byron F. Radebaugh, "A Preface to the Development of a Democratic Ethic," (Paper presented at the Annual Convention of the American Educational Studies Association, Pittsburgh, November 8, 1992): 4-6.

26. John R. Berrueta-Clement and others, *Changed Lives: The Effects of the Perry Preschool Program on Youths Through Age 19* (Ypsilanti, Michigan: High/Scope Educational Research Foundation, 1984); and Lawrence J. Schweinhart and David P. Weikart, "Success by Empowerment: The High/Scope Perry Preschool Study Through Age 27," *Young Children* 49, 1 (November 1993): 54-58.

27. Rick Heber, *Rehabilitation of Families at Risk for Mental Retardation* (Madison: University of Wisconsin Rehabilitation Center, 1968); Howard Gaber and Rick Heber, *The Milwaukee Project: Early Intervention As A Technique to Prevent Mental Retardation* (Storrs: University of Connecticut, Storrs National Leadership Institute, 1973).

28. Gary Wills, *Inventing America: Jefferson's Declaration of Independence* (Garden City: Doubleday and Company, Inc., 1978): 299-301.

29. Charles E. Lindblom, *Politics and Markets: The World's Political-Economic Systems* (New York: Basic Books, Inc., 1977).

30. *Ibid.*, 5.

31. *Ibid.*, 356.

GLOSSARY

Acculturation The process by which individuals adapt to a dominant culture other than their own.

Anglo-Conformity An ideological system which demands that all citizens renounce their ancestral cultures in favor of the behavior and values of the Anglo-Saxon core group.

Anglo-Conformist Education Schooling which socializes all students into the anglo-centric mainstream by demanding adoption of the language, attitudes, behaviors, and beliefs of the Anglo-Saxon core culture and the renunciation of other ancestral cultures.

Anthropic Cosmological Principle Human intelligence is essential not only to the nature of the universe, but to its very existence, and our existence accounts for at least some of the characteristics of the universe around us. *Anthropic* means "of humankind" and *cosmological* pertains to the study of the universe as a whole.

Assimilation The process by which individuals relinquish their cultural traits and acquire the traits of the mainstream culture.

Biculturalism The ability to operate effectively in two different cultures.

Bidialectal The ability to speak two dialects (e.g. standard and non-standard English) fluently.

Bilingual The ability to speak two languages fluently.

Business as Usual According to Sleeter and Grant, this is traditional, teacher-centered education which favors maintaining the anglo-centric status quo with little accommodation to different student learning styles or individualization.

Corporate Pluralism A social organization in which racial and ethnic groups are given official standing and economic and political rewards are allocated on a numerical basis. Equality of condition is emphasized, and structural and cultural pluralism are officially encouraged.

Corporately Pluralistic Multicultural Education Schooling which sensitizes majority group children to cultures other than their own and engages children of subordinate groups in critical analyses of their group's condition. The children of subordinate groups are empowered by the development of conceptual skills to resist oppression by the dominant group and are encouraged to become socially active in righting the social inequities which exist in the society.

Cultural Disadvantage A situation in which a person from a different culture finds himself or herself in a cultural context which places those whose language, behaviors, attitudes and/or values are different from the norm in an unfavorable position.

Culturally Different Individuals who exist within a cultural context different from their own.

Cultural Pluralism A social arrangement through which different cultural groups within a society participate fully and equally in the total life of the society, while maintaining their cultural identities.

Culture The total way of life of a people and all those aspects of living like language, religion, rituals, diets, values, and attitudes which influence their behavior and make them distinctive.

Education that is Multicultural and Social Reconstructionist According to Sleeter and Grant, this is an approach to education that attempts to promote social structural equality and cultural pluralism in the society by preparing future citizens to work actively toward these goals.

Enculturation The process by which individuals learn and internalize their cultures by interacting with their families, churches, friends, and other social agents who share the same language, attitudes, values, and beliefs.

Ethclass Each person is a member of an ethnic group and a social class. A person's sense of identity is related to these memberships, with social class being the more important of the two. In personal relationships people tend to be closest to members of their own social class within their own ethnic group.

Ethnic Group A group of people who share a sense of peoplehood stemming from history. They have a common social-psychological core based on race, religion, and national heritage.

Ethnic Studies An orientation to learning which utilizes the sense of identity gained by a people from the same national heritage group, religion, race, and nation who, by sharing a sense of peoplehood, have a common social-psychological conceptual reference point. This shared social-psychological reference point is utilized in the study of a range of phenomena throughout a curriculum and is not limited to a particular discipline. A multiethnic curriculum would, for instance, study every aspect of the world through the multiple models of reality provided by alternative ethnic perspectives. Ethnic studies also involves a multidisciplinary study of ethnic groups themselves, their histories, literature, art, philosophies, etc.

Ethnocentrism The view that one's own group is the center of everything, and all others are scaled and rated with reference to it. The point of view that one's own way of life is to be preferred to all others.

Hegemony The dominance of one group by another, especially where the dominance-subordinance relationship is connected to the subordinate group's acceptance of the dominant group's social assumptions.

Human Relations According to Sleeter and Grant, this educational approach tries to promote feelings of unity, tolerance, and acceptance among people within the existing social structure.

Ideology The belief system of a group, based on an interpretation of the group's past, which leads to prescriptions for present and future social policy. The ideological interpretation of the past may or may not be historically accurate, but the social assumptions it generates provide an orientation for the group in all areas of life.

Liberal Pluralism A social organization characterized by the absence of any legal or governmental recognition of racial, religious, language, or national origins and the prohibition of the use of ethnic criteria for discriminatory or for favored treatment. Equality of opportunity is emphasized for individuals as well as freedom of ethnic group members to choose or not to choose structural or cultural pluralism at their will.

Liberally Pluralistic Multicultural Education Schooling which focuses on the development of critical thinking and problem solving by teaching students to become conversant with and able to use different cultural models of reality for analyzing issues. In this process student learning and language styles, values, attitudes, and beliefs are accommodated to. Cross-cultural communication, understanding, respect and collaborative problem solving are emphasized.

Mainstream Culture In the United States this is generally considered to be the way of life characterized by adherence to norms and values grounded in Western European, and especially Anglo-Saxon or Anglo Teutonic, traditions.

Marginal Person One who is forced to live in two antagonistic cultures and therefore fails to feel the identity expected of him or her.

Melting Pot Assimilation of diverse peoples through a biological merger which blends their cultures into a new American type.

Metacultural Transcending cultural encapsulation, rather than being trapped in any one cultural context.

Multicultural Education A school situation which reflects the cultural diversity of the nation and world in its social and school goals and curricular and instructional aims and practices. It accommodates to the cultural norms, values, attitudes, behaviors, language, and learning styles of students and teaches all students to understand and respect their own and other cultures through an integrated, multidisciplinary, multiethnic curriculum.

Oligopoly The control of an economic market by a small number of suppliers.

Polyarchy A system of social organization in which the control of authority is in the hands of the many. Top authority is assigned through elections in which any one citizen's vote is by some formula counted as equal to any other's.

Power Elite The approximately 7,000 persons in whose hands resides the power to direct social policy in the United States. They are those with leadership positions in the corporate establishment, government, and the military, which comprise a subtle dictatorship of an interlocking structure of power.

Race Differential concentrations of gene frequencies which account for skin color, hair form, and other physical characteristics. Race has no intrinsic connection with cultural patterns which are learned.

Significance of the Difference Between Percentages A statistical measure of the reliability of the difference in two or more independent samples. The hypothesis being tested with this statistic is that no true difference exists between the percentages. A refutation of this hypothesis at the .01 level means that there is only one chance in 100 that a difference of this size would be by chance. Ninety-nine times out of 100, with the independent sample sizes being taken into account, this is a true difference. The .05 level means that ninety-five times out of 100 this is a true difference, and so on.

Single-Group Studies According to Sleeter and Grant, this approach to schooling promotes social structural equality and immediate recognition for the group of which the student is a member. Faculty who are group members teach about the history of victimization the group has suffered and current issues facing the group. Utilizing the learning style of the group, they call on students to work for social change which would benefit their group.

Social Class The hierarchy of social status groups based on differences in economic and political power.

Structural Pluralism The condition of a society which is segregated along ethclass lines.

Teaching the Exceptional and Culturally Different According to Sleeter and Grant, this approach to education tries to fit students into the existing social structure and culture by making traditional subject matter relevent to students' experiential backgrounds.

REFERENCES

American Association of School Administrators. *American Association of School Administrators 1976 Platform*. Arlington: American Association of School Administrators, 1976.

Anderson, James A. "Cognitive Styles and Multicultural Populations." *Journal of Teacher Education* 39, 1 (January-February 1988): 2-9.

Anderson, James A. "Reaching Beyond Monoculturalism: Acknowledging the Demands of Diversity." *SAEOPP Journal* 8, 2 (1989).

Baker, Gwendolyn C. "Multicultural Training for Student Teachers." *Journal of Teacher Education* (Winter 1973): 306-307.

Banks, James A. *Teaching Ethnic Studies: Concepts and Strategies*, 43rd Yearbook. Washington, D.C.: National Council for the Social Studies, 1973.

Banks, James A., et. al. *Curriculum Guidelines for Multiethnic Education: Position Statement*. Arlington: National Council for the Social Studies, 1976.

Banks, James A. *Teaching Strategies for Ethnic Studies*, Fifth Edition. Boston: Allyn and Bacon, 1991.

Banks, James A. "Approaches to Multicultural Curriculum Reform." In *Multicultural Education: Issues and Perspectives*, Second Edition, edited by James A. Banks and Cherry A. McGee Banks, 195-214. Boston: Allyn and Bacon, 1993.

Banks, James A. "Multicultural Education: Characteristics and Goals." In *Multicultural Education: Issues and Perspectives*, Second Edition, edited by James A. Banks and Cherry A. McGee Banks, 3-28. Boston: Allyn and Bacon, 1993.

Banks, James A. *An Introduction to Multicultural Education*, Boston: Allyn and Bacon, 1994.

Banks, James A. *Multiethnic Education: Theory and Practice*, Third Edition. Boston: Allyn and Bacon, 1994.

Banks, James A. "Multicultural Education: Historical Development, Dimensions, and Practice." In *Handbook of Research on Multicultural Education*, edited by James A. Banks and Cherry A. McGee Banks, 3-24. New York: Simon and Schuster Macmillan, 1995.

Banks, James A. and Cherry A. McGee Banks, eds. *Multicultural Education: Issues and Perspectives*, Second Edition. Boston: Allyn and Bacon, 1993.

Banks, James A. and Cherry A. McGee Banks, eds. *Handbook of Research on Multicultural Education*. New York: Simon and Schuster Macmillan, 1995.

Bengelsdorf, Winnie. *Ethnic Studies in Higher Education: State of the Art and Bibliography*. Washington, D.C.: American Association of State Colleges and Universities, 1972.

Bennett, Kathleen P. and Margaret D. Lecompte. *How Schools Work: A Sociological Analysis of Education*. New York: Longman, 1990.

Bennett, William J. *Our Children and Our Country: Improving America's Schools and Affirming the Common Culture*. New York: Simon and Schuster, 1988.

Berrueta-Clement, John R., et. al. *Changed Lives: The Effects of the Perry Preschool Program on Youths Through Age 19*. Ypsilanti, Michigan: High/Scope Educational Research Foundation, 1984 (ERIC ED 313 128).

Bloom, Allan. *The Closing of the American Mind*. New York: Simon and Schuster, 1987.

Bonutti, Karl B. "Ethnic Studies — Another Experiment or Just a Belated Beginning?" *Momentum* 6, 3 (1975): 41-45.

Bowen, Ella M. and Frederick L. Salsman. "Internship in Integration." *Nation's Schools and Colleges* (March 1975): 30, 31.

Bowen, Ella M. and Frederick L. Salsman. "Integrating Multiculturalism into a Teacher Training Program." *Journal of Negro Education* (Summer 1979): 390-395.

Caselli, R. "Ethnic Studies—Opportunity to Revitalize Education." *Contemporary Education* 42, 6 (1971): 301-304.

Cheney, Lynne V. *American Memory: A Report on the Humanities in the Nation's Public Schools*. Washington, D.C.: National Endowment for the Humanities, 1987.

Cheney, Lynne V. *Tyrannical Machines: A Report on Educational Practices Gone Wrong and Our Best Hopes for Setting Them Straight*. Washington, D.C.: National Endowment for the Humanities, 1990.

Chilcott, John H. "An Analysis of the Enculturation of Values as Illustrated in Primary Readers, 1879-1960." Paper presented at the meeting of the California Educational Research Association, Palo Alto, March 4, 1961.

Clarke, Anthony. "Ethnic Studies: Reflection and Re-Examination." *Journal of Negro Education* 46, 2 (1977): 124-132.

Cole, Stewart G. and Mildred Wiese Cole. *Minorities and the American Promise*. New York: Harper and Brothers, 1954.

Cortes, Carlos with Fay Metcalf and Sherryl Hawke. *Understanding You and Them: Tips for Teaching About Ethnicity*. Boulder: Social Science Education Consortium, Inc., 1976.

Council of Chief State School Officers. *1975 Policy Statements of the Council of Chief State School Officers*. Washington, D.C.: Council of Chief State School Officers, 1975.

Counts, George S. *The Social Foundations of Education*. New York: Charles Scribner's Sons, 1934.

Crouchett, Lawrence P. "The Merger of Ethnic Studies and General Education." *The Journal of Ethnic Studies* 6, 2 (1978): 35-48.

Cummins, J. "Empowering Minority Students: A Framework for Intervention." *Harvard Educational Review* 56 (Spring 1986): 18-36.

de Tocqueville, Alexis. *Democracy in America*, edited by J. P. Mayer and Max Lerner, translated by George Lawrence. New York: Harper and Row, 1966.

Dewey, John. "Nationalizing Education." In *Addresses and Proceedings of the Fifty-fourth Annual Meeting*, 185-186. National Education Association of the United States, 1916.

D'Souza, Dinesh. *Illiberal Education: The Policies of Race and Sex on Campus.* New York: The Free Press, 1991.

Farquhar, Elizabeth. "Title IX: The Ethnic Heritage Studies Program—The 'What' and 'How To'." *Momentum* 6 (October 1975): 46-50.

Gambino, Richard. *A Guide to Ethnic Studies Programs in American Colleges, Universities, and Schools.* New York: The Rockefeller Foundation Working Papers, 1975.

Garber, Howard and Rick Heber. *The Milwaukee Project: Early Intervention As A Technique to Prevent Mental Retardation.* Storrs: University of Connecticut, Storrs National Leadership Institute, 1973.

Gibbs, C. R. "Project 2000: Why Black Men Should Teach Black Boys" *Dollars and Sense* (February/March 1991): 19-27.

Giles, Raymond H. and Donna M. Gollnick. "Ethnic/Cultural Diversity As Reflected in Federal and State Educational Legislation and Policies." In *Pluralism and the American Teacher: Issues and Case Studies*, edited by Frank H. Klassen and Donna M. Gollnick, 115-160. Washington D.C.: Ethnic Heritage Center for Teacher Education of the American Association of Colleges for Teacher Education, 1977.

Giroux, H. *Theory and Resistance in Education: A Pedagogy for the Opposition.* South Hadley, Massachusetts: Bergin and Garvey, 1983.

Giroux, H. "Critical Pedagogy, Cultural Politics and the Discourse of Experience." *Journal of Education* 167, 1 (1985): 22-41.

Giroux, H. "Literacy and the Pedagogy of Voice and Political Empowerment." *Educational Theory* 38 (1988): 61-75.

Gollnick, Donna M. "National and State Initiatives for Multicultural Education." In *Handbook of Research on Multicultural Education*, edited by James A. Banks and Cherry A. McGee Banks, 44-64. New York: Simon and Schuster Macmillan, 1995.

Gollnick, Donna M. and Philip C. Chinn. *Multicultural Education in a Pluralistic Society.* Columbus: Merril Publishing Company, 1990.

Gollnick, Donna M., Frank H. Klassen and Joost Yff. *Multicultural Education and Ethnic Studies in the United States: An Analysis and Annotated Bibliography of Selected Documents in ERIC.* Washington, D.C.: American Association of Colleges for Teacher Education, 1976.

Gordon, Milton M. *Assimilation in American Life.* New York: Oxford University Press, 1964.

Gordon, Milton M. *Human Nature, Class, and Ethnicity.* New York: Oxford University Press, 1978.

Grant, Carl A., ed. *Educating for Diversity: An Anthology of Multicultural Voices.* Boston: Allyn and Bacon, 1995.

Greenbaum, William. "America in Search of a New Ideal: An Essay on the Rise of Pluralism." *Harvard Educational Review* 44, 3 (August 1974): 411-440.

Greene, Victor. "Old Ethnic Stereotypes and the New Ethnic Studies." *Ethnicity* 5, 4 (1978): 328-350.

Haller, Elizabeth S. *New Perspectives: A Bibliography of Racial, Ethnic and Feminist Resources.* Harrisburg: Pennsylvania Department of Education, 1977.

Harrington, Michael. *The Other America.* Baltimore: Penguin Books, Inc., 1971.

Heber, Rick. *Rehabilitation of Families At Risk for Mental Retardation.* Madison: University of Wisconsin Rehabilitation Center, 1968.

Hirsch, Jr., E. D. *Cultural Literacy: What Every American Needs to Know.* Boston: Houghton Mifflin Company, 1987.

Hirsch, Jr., E. D. *The Dictionary of Cultural Literacy: What Every American Needs to Know.* Boston: Houghton Mifflin Company, 1988.

Hirsch, Jr., E. D. *A First Dictionary of Cultural Literacy.* Boston: Houghton Mifflin Company, 1989.

Holland, Spencer, et. al. *Project 2000.* Baltimore: Center for Educating African-American Males, Morgan State University's School of Education and Urban Studies, 1990.

Hook, Sidney. *Reason, Social Myths and Democracy.* New York: The John Day Company, 1940.

Hunter, William A., ed. *Multicultural Education Through Competency Based Teacher Education.* Washington, D.C.: American Association of Colleges for Teacher Education, 1974.

Kallen, Horace M. *Culture and Democracy in the United States.* New York: Boni and Liveright, 1924.

Kallen, Horace M. *Cultural Pluralism and The American Idea.* Philadelphia: University of Pennsylvania Press, 1956.

Kelly, Fern. "A System Approaches Multicultural Education." *Educational Leadership* 32 (December 1974): 183-186.

Kolack, Shirley. "A Course in Ethnic Studies." *Teaching Sociology* 3, 1 (1975): 60-73.

Krug, Mark M. "Teaching the Experience of White Ethnic Groups." In *Teaching Ethnic Studies: Concepts and Strategies*, edited by James A. Banks. Washington, D.C.: National Council for the Social Studies 43rd Yearbook, 1973.

Lewis, Oscar. *The Children of Sanchez: Autobiography of a Mexican Family.* New York: Random House, 1961.

Lindblom, Charles E. *Politics and Markets: The World's Political-Economic Systems*. New York: Basic Books, Inc., 1977.

MacDonald, James B. "Cultural Pluralism As ASCD's Major Thrust." *Educational Leadership* 32 (December 1974): 167.

McCarthy, C. *Race and Curriculum: Social Inequality and the Theories and Politics of Difference in Contemporary Research on Schooling*. London: The Falmer Press, 1990.

McCarthy C. "Race and Education in the United States: The Multicultural Solution." *Interchange* 21 (1990): 45-55.

McConville, Lawrence J. *Ethnic Studies Curricula and Related Institutional Entities at Southwestern Colleges and Universities*. El Paso: The Cross-Cultural Southwest Ethnic Study Center, The University of Texas at El Paso, 1975.

McLaren, Peter. *Life in Schools: An Introduction to Critical Pedagogy in the Foundations of Education*. New York: Longman, 1989.

Minderhout, David J., Robert R. Solenberger, and David E. Washburn. "The Southwestern Indian Aesthetic and The White Man's Vision." *Minority Voices* 2, 1 (Spring 1978): 31-42.

National Association of Elementary School Principals. *National Association of Elementary School Principals 1975 Platform*. Arlington: National Association of Elementary School Principals, 1975.

National Association of Secondary School Principals. *Secondary Schools in a Changing Society. This We Believe*. Reston: National Association of Secondary School Principals, 1975.

National School Public Relations Association. *Black Studies in Schools*. Arlington: National School Public Relations Association, 1970.

Nelson, Murry. "Ethnic Studies Programs — Some Historical Antecedents." *Social Studies* 63, 3 (1977): 104-108.

New York Times. June 28, 1987, 40. "Iroquois Constitution: A Forerunner to Colonists' Democratic Principles."

Nieto, Sonia. *Affirming Diversity: The Sociopolitical Context of Multicultural Education*, Second Edition. New York: Longman, 1996.

Ohio Department of Education. *Providing K-12 Multicultural Curricular Experiences*. Columbus: Office of Equal Educational Opportunity, Ohio Department of Education, 1974.

Oliver, William. "Black Males and Social Problems: Prevention Through Afrocentric Socialization." *Journal of Black Studies* 19 (September 1989): 15-39.

Olneck, M. "The Recurring Dream: Symbolism and Ideology in Intercultural and Multicultural Education." *American Journal of Education* 98, 2 (1989): 145-174.

Pennsylvania, Commonwealth of. *Senate Bill No. 1618*, 1974, Act No. 322: 872.

Radebaugh, Byron F. "A Preface to the Development of a Democratic Ethic." Paper presented at the Annual Convention of the American Educational Studies Association, Pittsburgh, November 8, 1992.

Ratner, Joseph, ed. *Intelligence in the Modern World: John Dewey's Philosophy.* New York: Random House, 1939.

Raymond, Chris. "Global Migration Will Have Widespread Impact on Society, Scholars Say." *The Chronicle of Higher Education* (September 12, 1990): A-1, 6.

Record, Jane Cassels and Wilson Record. "Ethnic Studies and Affirmative Action—Ideological Roots and Implications for Quality of American Life." *Social Science Quarterly* 55, 2 (1974): 502-519.

Sarup, M. *The Politics of Multiracial Education.* New York: Routledge and Kegan Paul, 1986.

Sayers, Ephraim Vern and Ward Madden. *Education and the Democratic Faith.* New York: Appleton, Century-Crofts, Inc., 1959.

Schweinhart, Lawrence J. and David P. Weikart. "Success by Empowerment: The High/Scope Perry Preschool Study Through Age 27." *Young Children* 49, 1 (November 1993): 54-58.

"A School for Black Males: Is It An Answer for Baltimore?" *The Abell Report* 2, 5 (January/February 1991): 1-4.

Silber, John. *Straight Shooting: What's Wrong With America and How to Fix It.* New York: Harper and Row, 1989.

Sleeter, Christine E. *Empowerment Through Multicultural Education.* Albany: State University of New York Press, 1991.

Sleeter, Christine E. and Carl A. Grant. *Making Choices for Multicultural Education: Five Approaches to Race, Class, and Gender.* Columbus: Merril Publishing Company, 1988.

Social Science Education Consortium, Inc. *Materials and Human Resources for Teaching Ethnic Studies.* Boulder: Social Science Education Consortium, Inc., 1975.

Sowers, Marjorie E. "Opportunity Week: Increasing Multicultural Awareness in A Teacher Education Program." *Teacher Educator* (Summer 1979): 32-36.

Spring, Joel. *Deculturalization and the Struggle for Equality: A Brief History of the Education of Dominated Cultures in the United States.* New York: McGraw-Hill, Inc., 1994.

Spring, Joel A. *The Intersection of Cultures: Multicultural Education in the United States.* New York: McGraw-Hill, Inc., 1995.

Steibel, Warren (producer). *Firing Line Special Debate—Resolved: Freedom of Thought is in Danger on American Campuses.* Public Broadcasting System in association with South Carolina Instructional Television, September 6, 1991.

Swiereng, R. P. "Ethnocultural Political Analysis—New Approach to American Ethnic Studies." *Journal of American Studies* 5, 1 (1971): 59-79.

Thompson, Bryan and Carol Agocs. "Ethnic Studies: Teaching and Research Needs." *Journal of Geography* 72 (1973): 13-23.

United States Department of Education. *Directory of Public Elementary and Secondary Education Agencies: 1992-93*. Washington, D.C.: National Center for Education Statistics, 1994.

van den Berghe, Pierre L. "The Present State of Comparative Race and Ethnic Studies." In *Problems in International Comparative Research in the Social Sciences*, edited by Jan Berting, Felix Geyer and Ray Jurkovich. New York: Pergamon Press, 1979.

Vickery, William E. and Stewart G. Cole. *Intercultural Education in American Schools*. New York and London: Harper and Brothers, 1943.

Villemain, Francis T. and Nathaniel Champlin. "Frontiers for an Experimentalist Philosophy of Education." In *Readings in Art Education*, edited by Elliot W. Eisner and David W. Ecker. Waltham: Blausdell Publishing Company, 1966.

Washburn, David E. *Democracy and the Education of the Disadvantaged: A Pragmatic Inquiry*. Portland, Oregon: Lewis and Clark College, 1971.

Washburn, David E. "A Conceptual Framework for Multicultural Education." *The Florida FL Reporter: A Journal of Language and Culture in Education* 10, 1 and 2 (Spring/Fall 1972): 27-28.

Washburn, David E. *Dexter, Pedro and Richard*. Miami: WTVJ Television News, March 26, 1972. 25 minutes, color, 16 mm film or video. Distributed by Inquiry International.

Washburn, David E. *The Basketmaker*. Philadelphia: Inquiry International Appalachian Life and Culture Series, 1974, black and white, video, 50 minutes.

Washburn, David E. *Coal is King: Stripmining in Kentucky*. Philadelphia: Inquiry International Appalachian Life and Culture Series, 1974, black and white video, 50 minutes.

Washburn, David E. *The Heritage of a Young Appalachian*. Philadelphia: Inquiry International Appalachian Life and Culture Series, 1974, black and white, video, 50 minutes.

Washburn, David E. *The Life and Times of Verna Mae Slone*. Philadelphia: Inquiry International Appalachian Life and Culture Series, 1974, black and white, video, 50 minutes.

Washburn, David E. *The Old Regular Baptists*. Philadelphia: Inquiry International Appalachian Life and Culture Series, 1974, black and white, video, 50 minutes.

Washburn, David E. *Politics in Knott County, Kentucky*. Philadelphia: Inquiry International Appalachian Life and Culture Series, 1974, black and white, video, 50 minutes.

Washburn, David E. "Growing in Pippa Passes." *Pennsylvania Education* 6, 1 (September 9, 1974): 3.

Washburn, David E. "Where to Find Ethnic Studies Materials." *Social Education* 39, 1 (January 1975): 40-41.

Washburn, David E. "Ethnic Studies in the United States." *Educational Leadership* 32, 6 (March 1975): 409-412.

Washburn, David E. "Multicultural Education in the United States." *Phi Delta Kappan* 56, 9 (May 1975): 636.

Washburn, David E. "The Pennsylvania Ethnic Heritage Studies Survey." *Pennsylvania Ethnic Studies Newsletter* 3, 1 (September 1977): 3-7.

Washburn, David E. "Multiethnic Education in Pennsylvania." *Phi Delta Kappan* 59, 8 (April 1978): 561.

Washburn, David E. "An Appalachian Summer." *Improving College and University Teaching* 26, 3 (Summer 1978): 192-193.

Washburn, David E. *Directory of Ethnic Studies in Pennsylvania.* Pittsburgh: University of Pittsburgh Center for International Studies, 1978.

Washburn, David E. *Ethnic Studies in Pennsylvania.* Pittsburgh: University of Pittsburgh Center for International Studies, 1978.

Washburn, David E. *Ethnic Studies, Bilingual/Bicultural Education and Multicultural Teacher Education in the United States: A Directory of Higher Education Programs and Personnel.* Miami: Inquiry International, 1979.

Washburn, David E. "Multicultural Education: Origins, Development and Prospects." *Research Bulletin* Florida Agricultural and Mechanical University 23, 1 (May 1979): 33-39.

Washburn, David E. *Multicultural Education Programs, Ethnic Studies Curricula, and Ethnic Studies Materials in the United States Public Schools.* Washington, D.C.: Educational Resources Information Center Clearinghouse on Teacher Education, 1980 (ED 180 944).

Washburn, David E. *Bilingual/Bicultural Education in the United States: Higher Education.* Washington, D.C.: Educational Resources Information Center Clearinghouse on Teacher Education, 1981 (ED 204 325).

Washburn, David E. *Ethnic Studies in the United States: Higher Education.* Washington, D.C.: Educational Resources Information Center Clearinghouse on Higher Education, 1981 (ED 206 232).

Washburn, David E. *Multicultural Education: A Chronological Bibliography of Selected Materials.* Washington, D.C.: Educational Resources Information Center Clearinghouse on Teacher Education, 1981 (ED 204 324).

Washburn, David E. *Multicultural Teacher Education in the United States.* Washington, D.C.: Educational Resources Information Center Clearinghouse on Teacher Education, 1981 (ED 204 326).

Washburn, David E. *The Peoples of Pennsylvania: An Annotated Bibliography of Resource Materials.* Pittsburgh: University of Pittsburgh Center for International Studies, 1981.

Washburn, David E. Review of "The Lattimer Tragedy of 1897," by George Turner. *Pennsylvania Heritage* 3, 3 (June 1977): 10-13. In *The Peoples of Pennsylvania: An Annotated Bibliography of Resource Materials*. Pittsburgh: University of Pittsburgh Center for International Studies, 1981, 189.

Washburn, David E. Review of *Pennsylvania: An Ethnic Portrait—Program One: Quakers, Germans, and Scots-Irish* by Martha Smith and Steven Smith. Scranton: Sandar Films/WVIA Television, 1976, color, video, 30 minutes. In *The Peoples of Pennsylvania: An Annotated Bibliography of Resource Materials*. Pittsburgh: University of Pittsburgh Center for International Studies, 1981, 52.

Washburn, David E. Review of *Pennsylvania: An Ethnic Portrait—Program Two: Welsh and Irish* by Martha Smith and Steven Smith. Scranton: Sandar Films/WVIA Television, 1976 color, video, 30 minutes. In *The Peoples of Pennsylvania: An Annotated Bibliography of Resource Materials*. Pittsburgh: University of Pittsburgh Center for International Studies, 1981, 52.

Washburn, David E. Review of *Pennsylvania: An Ethnic Portrait—Program Three: Italians and Jews* by Martha Smith and Steven Smith. Scranton: Sandar Films/WVIA Television, 1976, color, video, 30 minutes. In *The Peoples of Pennsylvania: An Annotated Bibliography of Resource Materials*. Pittsburgh: University of Pittsburgh Center for International Studies, 1981, 52-53.

Washburn, David E. Review of *Pennsylvania: An Ethnic Portrait—Program Four: Eastern Europeans* by Martha Smith and Steven Smith. Scranton: Sandar Films/WVIA Television, 1976 color, video, 30 minutes. In *The Peoples of Pennsylvania: An Annotated Bibliography of Resource Materials*. Pittsburgh: University of Pittsburgh Center for International Studies, 1981, 53.

Washburn, David E. Review of *Pennsylvania: An Ethnic Portrait—Program Five: Blacks and Puerto Ricans* by Martha Smith and Steven Smith. Scranton: Sandar Films/WVIA Television, 1976 color, video, 30 minutes. In *The Peoples of Pennsylvania: An Annotated Bibliography of Resource Materials*. Pittsburgh: University of Pittsburgh Center for International Studies, 1981, 53.

Washburn, David E. "Cultural Pluralism: Are Teachers Prepared?" *Phi Delta Kappan* 63, 7 (March 1982): 493-495.

Washburn, David E. Review of *Racism and Reaction: A Profile of Handsworth* by Peter Ratcliffe. *Educational Studies* (England) 8, 2 (1982): 165-166.

Washburn, David E. "Ethnic Studies in the United States: Higher Education." *CORE: An International Journal of Educational Research*, Carfax Publishing Company, Oxford, England 6, 3 (1982) Fiche 15 G 8.

Washburn, David E. "Pennsylvania." In *Book of Days 1987*, edited by C. Edward Wall and Clifford S. Johnson, 625-627. Ann Arbor: Pierian Press, 1986.

Washburn, David E., et. al. *Multicultural Understanding: A Resource Directory for the Wilkes-Barre and Hazleton Area School Districts*. Bloomsburg, Pennsylvania: Bloomsburg University of Pennsylvania, 1989.

Washburn, David E. "Reinventing the Social Foundations of Education." *Educational Foundations* 7, 4 (Fall 1993): 71-76.

Washburn, David E. "Let's Take A Hard Look at Multicultural Education." *Multicultural Education* 2, 2 (Winter 1994): 20-23.

Washburn, David E. *Multicultural Education Policy in the United States: A Social Foundations Analysis*. Eugene, Oregon: Educational Resources Information Center Clearinghouse on Educational Management, 1995 (ED 381 887).

Washburn, David E. *A Social Foundations Approach to Educational Policy Analysis*. Eugene, Oregon: Educational Resources Information Center Clearinghouse on Educational Management, 1995 (ED 383 052).

Washburn, David E. and Neil L. Brown. *The Multicultural Education Directory*. Philadelphia: Inquiry International, 1996.

Wills, Gary. *Inventing America: Jefferson's Declaration of Independence*. Garden City: Doubleday and Company, Inc., 1978.

ACKNOWLEDGMENTS

The 1995 survey of the 713 largest school districts in the United States on which a portion of this book is based was partially supported with a grant from the Bloomsburg University of Pennsylvania Faculty Professional Development Fund. However, the opinions expressed herein do not necessarily represent the position or policy of the Bloomsburg University of Pennsylvania Faculty Professional Development Committee, and no official endorsement by Bloomsburg University of Pennsylvania is implied or should be inferred.

We would like to thank the following persons who assisted in the development and production of this work: Sam, Ginny, and Cade Bidleman, Deanne Ferguson, Faith G. Kline, Daniel C. Washburn, David T. Washburn, and Maria Christian Workman.

INDEX

A

academic freedom 19
acculturation 3, 4, 78, 115 (*defined*)
affirmative action 34
African Americans 10, 11, 14, 24, 26, 27-29,
    32-34, 36, 51, 52, 86
afrocentrism 24
Albany Congress 78
alternative assessment 91
America (or *Goals*) *2000* 20, 76
American Association of Colleges for
    Teacher Education 13
American Association of School
    Administrators 13
American core culture 20
American Dream 4, 13
Amish 28
anglo-centrism 79, 80, 115
anglo-conformist 14, 19-21, 55, 74-78, 91,
    115 (*defined*)
anglo-conformity 18, 76, 77, 79, 80, 90, 115
Anglo-Saxon 8-10, 18, 77, 78, 115, 117
Anglo-Teutonic 37, 77
anglocentrism 78
anthropic cosmological principle 77, 115
    (*defined*)
Arab Americans 37
Arizona 49
Arkansas 12, 76
Asian Americans 10, 32, 36
Asian languages 11, 33, 51
Asian/Pacific Islander American 51, 52
aspects of the classroom 42, 53, 55, 81, 85,
    100
assessment 85, 91
assimilation 1, 3, 4, 8, 9, 14, 18, 20, 26, 76-
    81, 90, 107, 112, 115 (*defined*), 118
Association for Supervision and Curriculum
    Development 13

B

Banks, James A. 21, 74, 106, 108-112, 121,
    123, 124
Bengelsdorf, Winnie 110, 121
Bennett (deMarrais), Kathleen P. *see* Bennett
    and Lecompte
Bennett, William J. 14, 19, 108, 121, 122
Bennett and Lecompte 82, 112

bicultural 3-5, 10, 11, 30-33, 56
bicultural curriculum 10
biculturalism 115 (*defined*)
bidialectal 3, 23, 115 (*defined*)
bilingual 3, 10, 11, 16, 23, 30-33, 38, 51, 56,
    115 (*defined*)
bilingual curriculum 10
bilingual education 11, 16, 38
bilingual/bicultural education 11, 30-33
bilingualism 17
Bloom, Allan 14, 19, 28, 93, 96, 108, 122,
    129
Bush, George 14, 19, 76
business as usual 15, 16, 19, 74, 76, 115
    (*defined*)

C

California 12, 32, 35, 49, 50
Canassatego 78
Cantonese 33
capitalism 79, 88, 89
Center for the Education of African American
    Males 24
Central United States 49, 50, 57, 77
Central American 33
central-, eastern-, and southern-European 37,
    74
certification requirements 5
Champlain, Nathaniel *see* Villemain and
    Champlain
Cheney, Lynne V. 19, 108, 122
Cherokee 33
Chicanos 34
Chilcott, John H. 9, 105, 122
Chinese Americans 11, 28, 33
Choctaw 33
civil rights 9, 21
Civil Rights Movement 21
class size 87
classroom decorations 55-57
Clinton, Bill 76
collaborative economic models 88, 91
Commonwealth of Pennsylvania 11, 28, 29
community involvement 10, 23, 26, 27, 30,
    32, 35, 36, 41, 51, 52, 56, 57, 59 (*table*),
    98
community relations 10, 51
computer literate 88

DAVID E. WASHBURN is professor and coordinator of educational foundations at Bloomsburg University of Pennsylvania. He holds the B.A., M.Ed., and Ph.D. degrees from the University of Arizona and the post-doctoral certificate in multicultural education from the University of Miami. He is the author of sixteen books and monographs, including *Democracy and the Education of the Disadvantaged: A Pragmatic Inquiry*, *Ethnic Studies in Pennsylvania*, *Directory of Ethnic Studies in Pennsylvania*, *The Peoples of Pennsylvania*, *Ethnic Studies*, *Bilingual/Bicultural Education and Multicultural Teacher Education in the United States*, and *The Theoretical Foundations of Teaching and Learning*. With Neil L. Brown, he co-authored *The Multicultural Education Directory*. Among his numerous other works are publications which have appeared in *Multicultural Education*, *Educational Foundations*, *Educational Studies* (U.S.), *Educational Studies* (England), *CORE* (England), *Phi Delta Kappan*, the *Reasearch Bulletin* of Florida A & M University, *Pennsylvania Ethnic Studies Newsletter*, *Improving College and University Teaching*, *Minority Voices*, *Educational Leadership*, *Social Education*, *The Florida FL Reporter*, *Pennsylvania Education*, *Western Review*, *Book of Days 1987*, *America: History and Life*, and *The Journal of Global Awareness*. He has also written and produced a number of documentary films and videos, including *Dexter, Pedro, and Richard* for WTVJ Television, Miami, Florida.

NEIL L. BROWN is assistant professor of education at Bloomsburg University of Pennsylvania. He earned the Ed.D. in early childhood education from Temple University and conducts much of his research in the area of social studies education. The author of several texts and articles, his most recent publications include *Social Studies for Elementary Children in the 21st Century* and "Persisting and Common Stereotypes in U.S. Students' Knowledge of Africa: A Study of Preservice Social Studies Teachers" (co-author), published in *The Social Studies*.

ROBERT W. ABBOTT is director of academic computing at Bloomsburg University of Pennsylvania. He holds the B.A. and M.A. degrees from the University of Delaware and has particular expertise in statistical computing. Some of his most recent publications have appeared in *Administrative Computing in Higher Education*, *Campus-Wide Information Systems*, and *The Journal of Global Awareness*. He was visiting lecturer at Shenyang Teachers College in China during the summer of 1993.